THE WAY BACK

George Moore's *The Untilled Field* and *The Lake*

THE APPRAISAL SERIES
Irish and English Literature in Context
General Editor: Maurice Harmon

APPRAISAL

IRISH AND
ENGLISH LITERATURE
IN CONTEXT

SERIES

The APPRAISAL series presents, in one volume, *the key essays* — critical, inter-pretive or contextual — dealing with specific works of literature. These essays may be entirely original, being specially commissioned for the series where the editor considers existing material to be inadequate; or may bring together in a re-edited and structured volume, the most important essays for a full, and up-to-date, evaluation of the work; or, the APPRAISAL volume may combine both of these approaches, in order to achieve the best result.

Individual volumes in the APPRAISAL series are researched, edited and introduced by writers whose academic and scholarly expertise on their own subject is already established.

The General Editor for the series is Maurice Harmon of University College, Dublin.

Published in the series:
The Way Back: George Moore's The Untilled Field *and* The Lake
Editor: Robert Welch, University of Leeds

Forthcoming
Alive! Alive-O! Flann O'Brien's At Swim Two Birds
Editor: Rudiger Imhof, University of Wuppertal

Reading Maria Edgeworth's Castle Rackrent
Editor: Coilin Owens, George Mason University

Other volumes in preparation.

The Way Back
GEORGE MOORE'S
THE UNTILLED FIELD & THE LAKE

Editor

Robert Welch

BARNES & NOBLE BOOKS
Totowa, New Jersey

First published in the USA 1982 by
BARNES & NOBLE BOOKS
81 Adams Drive,
Totowa, New Jersey, 07512
in association with Wolfhound Press, Dublin
ISBN 0-389-20318-1

© 1982 Wolfhound Press
Introduction, Selection and Editing ©1982 Robert Welch
Essays© individual contributors and Wolfhound Press

Library of Congress Cataloging in Publication Data
Main entry under title:

The Way back.

    (Appraisal series)
    1. Moore, George, 1852-1933——Criticism and interpre-
tation——Addresses, essays, lectures. 2. Moore, George,
1852-1933. Untilled field——Addresses, essays, lectures.
3. Moore, George, 1852-1923. Lake——Addresses, essays,
lectures. 4. Ireland in literature——Addresses, essays,
lectures. I. Welch, Robert, 1947-   . II. Series.
PR5044.W3 1982 823'.8   82-11449
ISBN 0-389-20318-1

Cover design: Jarlath Hayes
Typesetting: Print Prep Ltd. Dublin.

CONTENTS

ACKNOWLEDGEMENTS

My thanks go to the following individuals and institutions who helped towards the production of this book: Prof. John Barnard, University of Leeds; Mr. Rivers Carew, Co. Meath; Mrs. Hilary Carey (née Pyle) of Cork; *Éire-Ireland*, St. Paul, Minnesota; Prof. Helmut E. Gerber of Arizona State University; Dr. Maurice Harmon of University College, Dublin; Mrs. Hollick of the University of Leeds; Prof. A.N. Jeffares of the University of Stirling; Prof. Brendan Kennelly of Trinity College (Dublin); Mr. Rory McTurk of the University of Leeds; the School of English, University of Leeds; Mr. Colin Smythe of Gerrards Cross; Dr. Michael Solomons of Dublin; Miss A.C. Stead of the University of Leeds; the Brotherton Library, University of Leeds; the British Library (London and Thorp Arch); Dundee Public Library; the National Library of Ireland; Trinity College (Dublin) Library; University College Library, Dublin; University College Library, Galway; and the University of Illinois Library.

For permission to print from George Moore's works I am grateful to Mr. J.C. Medley, executor of the George Moore estate, and to Mr. Colin Smythe.

Mo bhuíochas agus mo ghradh, ar deireadh, do mo bhean chéile, Angela, a foilsíonn fáth agus aidhm na h-oibre.

Robert Welch
Leeds

... we no longer know what is at stake in language. Because the destiny of language is grounded in a nation's *relation* to *being*, the question of being will involve us deeply in the question of language.

Heidegger

PREFACE

I

After years in Paris and in London Moore returned to Ireland in 1901. He was 49, a bit old, one might think, for enthusiasm, but was excited by the changes he saw taking place in the imaginative life of Ireland.

One of the qualities that Moore continually displays in his writing career is a kind of innocent openness to possibility. This is certainly to be discerned in his complex, passionate, often hilarious relations with the different aspects of the Gaelic and literary revivals which he had come back to augment. He wanted to take part in what he saw, at first, as a movement away from the sterile imperialism of England and the English, towards the more spontaneous life that Ireland seemed to offer. English itself seemed to be a language slackened by abstraction and commerce, whereas Irish was vivid, fresh, untainted by the exhaustion of modernity.

It is difficult for us now, bleakly accustomed as we are to the destructiveness of enthusiasm, to imagine the kind of excitement generated by the idea of the revival of the Irish language in the 1890s. Through the efforts of Douglas Hyde and others, it was no longer the badge of misery and failure, but became a symbol of the Irish identity consciously seeking cohesion between the past and the present, between different parts of itself, some of them lost or mislaid, some just neglected. The Gaelic League occasioned a kind of gathering together of memories, energies and emotions, that history had seemed to make disparate; it was the cultural emergence of the kind of nationhood that Young Ireland had striven for politically in the 1840s.

7

Moore had no Irish, of course, but he thought that his talents as a writer of fiction should be put at the service of the language revival movement. Irish life was, to a large extent, an 'untilled field' ('úrghort'), and the work of the writer of fiction was to break it open, revealing depth and the possibility of fruitfulness. He wanted to open into the essential, hitherto hidden, life of Ireland in the way that Turgenev, without commentary or moralising, revealed the essential life of Russia in his stories.[1]

A vital stage in this breaking of new ground was to be the translation of his original stories into Irish by 'Tórna' and Pádraig Ó Súilleabháin, which would re-vivify them, cleansing them of the exhaustion of modern English, thereby bringing them closer to the essential life of Ireland.

Naturally enough, this essential quality proved elusive. The resolution of the difficulty lay not in his going the whole way and learning Irish (he thought he was too old for that), but in finding a story in which that very elusiveness would be the main theme. The story is *The Lake*; its theme is the 'essential life' of the central character, the priest, Fr. Gogarty, which is ambiguous and constantly changing, so that his inner life is mysterious and puzzling to himself. Moore's prose suggests a mind slowly emerging into awareness of itself, in a lonely context of sky and lake water; ruined abbeys; fragmented memories of histories, legend and superstition; poverty; private shame and public disgrace; and news of possibility in the great world beyond the parish.

II

The essays gathered here constitute a searching inquiry into why it mattered to Moore that he should return to Ireland in the early years of this century, and into the first two works that came out of his homecoming, *The Untilled Field* and *The Lake*. Matters dealt with include: the writing of *The Untilled Field* and the ambitions he had for that collection; the relationship between the stories and *The Lake*; how he made use of

techniques associated with other artists to achieve his aims
— Turgenev and Wagner, for example; what the writing of
these two works showed him about the possibilities of style
in suggesting the movements of consciousness, and the
implications of that for his later writing. What is never in
doubt is Moore's inventiveness as a story-teller and his
seriousness as a craftsman.

III

These essays (apart from that by Max Cordonnier and the
short piece by John Cronin) are all newly commissioned. My
first intention was to ransack all the journals and reprint the
best work on these two books, but the simple fact was that
apart from some recent work by Richard Allen Cave and
John Cronin there is very little really good critical writing
anywhere on these crucial works of Moore's Irish period. It
seemed pointless to reprint from Cave's *A Study of the Novels
of George Moore* (Gerrards Cross, 1978). John Cronin's
valuable essay on *The Untilled Field* in *The Irish Short Story*
(Gerrards Cross, 1979), edited by Patrick Rafroidi and
Terence Brown, is also recent and easily available. Both Cave
and Cronin are contributors to this volume; the former's
piece being newly commissioned, the latter's being a reprint
of a short but interesting article on a possible source for the
story of *The Lake* from *Éire-Ireland* (Fall, 1971).
    Wherever it seemed appropriate I have introduced into the
annotations to the pieces gathered here references to those
essays in journals which the reader may find useful. A complete
bibliography of writings about Moore is being prepared by
Helmut E. Gerber for The Annotated Secondary Bibliography
Series from Northern Illinois University Press. This revises
and updates Gerber's own 'George Moore: An Annotated
Bibliography of Writings About Him', *English Fiction* (now
Literature) *in Transition*, II, 2, parts i and ii (1959), 1-91,
supplemented by additions in various issues thereafter.
    Gerber's *George Moore in Transition: Letters to T. Fisher*

Unwin and Lena Milman, 1894-1910 (Detroit, 1968), with the editor's useful commentary on the correspondence, has done much to improve our understanding of Moore during the Irish period. The same author's forthcoming *George Moore on Parnassus: Letters (1900-1933)* will put us further in his debt.

IV

All references to *The Untilled Field*, *The Lake* and *Hail and Farewell* throughout these essays are to the recent reprints published by Colin Smythe. Those of *The Lake* (1980) and *Hail and Farewell* (1976) are especially useful; the former has a comprehensive and illuminating afterword by Richard Allen Cave, while the latter has an introduction and extensive annotations by the same writer, which tell us much about Moore's Irish period.

V

For a variety of reasons Moore's position in modern Irish literary tradition has been an uncertain one. Yeats's hostility on the publication of *Hail and Farewell* (1911-1914) did not help. His own autobiography (begun a few months after the last volume of Moore's appeared, in 1914) has been, up to very recently, the official history of the literary movement. There has been a tendency to assent to the authority of the Yeatsian pronouncements on characters and events. This has meant that there has been insufficient attention to the pliant subtleties of Moore's narrative art, the sense that it gives of an alliance with the complicated movements of life.

Moore has always been difficult to categorize, and the simplest way of dealing with what cannot be categorized is to ignore it, or to convert your ignorance into the righteousness

of irritation. Moore has often been seen in Ireland as something
of a figure of fun, a slanting nincompoop, with lank hair and
limp hands. This caricature owes something to Yeats (who,
after all, had some reason to be irritated, Moore having compared him to an umbrella left behind at a party), and to Max
Beerbohm, but it also derives from the fact that Moore posed
some very difficult questions about the nature of Irish life. He
examined its quality of human sympathy, of true Christianity,
and found it wanting. He probed its spiritual life and found a
sterility under the piety. He analysed the dreams of cultural
regeneration in Ireland and found much obsessive egoism. A
difficult man, but he was a difficult man to himself as well as
to others. He did not fail to subject himself to the rigour of
his own mocking laughter. His integrity makes him nobody's
fool but his own. Such a self-sufficiency brings out the Irish
talent for detraction, a talent noted by Evelyn Waugh in a
letter to Nancy Mitford in 1952, having listened to a broad-
cast commemorating the centenary of Moore's birthday:

> They had been at work on it for years, collecting reports
> from everyone who had ever known him from the
> groom at Moore Park to Dublin literary colleagues. One
> after another the cracked old Irish voices took up the
> tale for nearly two hours, each demolishing bit by bit
> every corner of his reputation.[2]

Since Waugh wrote this Moore's international reputation
has risen steadily.[3] Now, with the wealth of information his
American bibliographer (Edwin Gilcher) and the editor of his
correspondence (Helmut E. Gerber) have made available to
us; equipped with the new reprints of the Irish works from
Colin Smythe; and stimulated by Cave's reading of the novels,
we are ready to attend to the deep humanity and artistic
inventiveness of the two related works that are the subject of
this collection of essays.

VI

The appendix reprints the same extract from different versions of the story which came to be known as 'The Wedding Gown' in *The Untilled Field*. These extracts show Moore making a real attempt to gain some kind of access to the Irish language by having his story translated, then allowing it to be re-translated back into English by T.W. Rolleston. They also display an impressive readiness to work and re-work.

Robert Welch

GEORGE MOORE'S GAELIC LAWN PARTY

Declan Kiberd

'Strike a blow for Irish by speaking it', urged Eoin Mac Neill in an address to the first recruits of the Gaelic League, adding the afterthought that 'if we cannot learn Irish we can at least stand up for it'. The history of Ireland in the decades after the foundation of the League in 1893 was to prove how much easier Mac Neill's second option was than his first. The brief career of George Moore as a leader of the Gaelic revival provides an apt and amusing illustration of that point.

It was a campaign which began, as all campaigns should, in a garret in London just one year after Mac Neill's rallying cry. One evening Moore's friend Edward Martyn expressed regret that he did not know enough Irish to write his plays in the language. Moore was astounded and remarked derisively to his friend: 'I thought nobody did anything in Irish except bring turf from the bog and say prayers.'[1] Martyn was the first Anglo-Irish writer to give serious consideration to the possibility of employing Irish as a literary medium, but the nearest he ever came to his ideal was in his drama *The Enchanted Sea*, whose hero speaks fluent Irish, but only offstage. Despite his initial misgivings, Moore was soon excited by the possibility of Ireland 'awakening at last out of the great sleep of Catholicism'. As he strode restlessly along the King's Bench Walk in the following days, he fantasised about 'writing a book in a new language or in the old language revived and sharpened to literary usage for the first time' (*Hail and Farewell*, p. 56). The reasons for his sudden enthusiasm were more personal than patriotic, for he had despaired of ever writing another creative work in English, a declining language which was 'losing its verbs' and in which 'everything had been already written' (p. 84). The noble idioms of Shakespeare could never be equalled, having been passed 'through the patty-pans of Stevenson into the pint-pot of Mr. Kipling'.[2] Moore was convinced that primitive peoples invented languages and that journalists destroyed them. He laid his curse on the journalists of England and decided to campaign for Irish, a language which had not been debased by abstract thought.

In that sense, the return to Irish might also be seen as an advance towards the modernism of Ezra Pound, who would soon revile journalists with his credo 'No ideas but in things'. From Yeats, Moore soon learned that there were no ideas in early Irish literature, only things: 'through dialect one escapes from abstract words, back to the sensation inspired directly by the thing itself' (p. 246). Knowing no Irish, Yeats was happy to study the concrete images and homely idioms of the Hiberno-English dialect, but such half measures could not satisfy Moore. Taking his cue from Edward Martyn, he denounced the dialect as a shoddy compromise: 'I like the English language and I like the Irish, but I hate the mixture' (p. 333). He was scathing in his rejection of Lady Gregory's 'Kiltartan whistle'; 'a dozen turns of speech' which could be easily emulated by any journalistic parrot (p. 550). Synge was scarcely any better, though Moore did pay him the compliment of parodying his idiom and his celebrated Parisian encounter with Yeats, who is caused to advise: 'Give up your schoolmaster words that have no guts left in them, and leave off thinking of Loti and his barley-sugar, and go down into County Wicklow and listen to what the people do be saying to 'other when they're at ease without any notion of an ear cocked to carry off what they say'.[3] All of which simply proves that Moore could never have mastered the dialect, so he preferred to denounce it in accordance with the approved policies of the Gaelic League.

'I came to give Ireland back her language', he remarked shortly after his return to the capital, and the cynics of literary Dublin wondered just how long it would take Ireland to give the native language back to George Moore. In the event their disbelief was justified, as he settled for Mac Neill's second option. Though he struggled through some early lessons, he soon abandoned the enterprise. Yeats uncharitably put it down to weakness of character: 'He did not go to Mass because his flesh was unwilling, as it was a year later when the teacher, engaged to teach him Gaelic, was told that he was out.'[4] His attempts to reform Irish cooking were no more successful and after a vicious argument as to the correct preparation of omelettes, his cook promptly resigned and called a policeman. Increasingly, the door at Ely Place went unanswered.

But Moore did speak up for Irish, with an intensity that bordered on absurdity, with a sincerity that seemed to many to come very close to parody. Having failed to master the language, he invested his hopes in the younger generation. 'That one child should learn Irish interests me far more than the production of a masterpiece',[5] he wrote in a letter to Yeats. At a meeting in February 1900 he explained his position: 'I have no children and am too old to learn the language, but I shall arrange at once that my brother's children shall learn Irish. I have written to my sister-in-law telling her that I will at once undertake this essential part of her children's education. They shall have a nurse straight from Aran; for it profits a man nothing if he knows all the languages of the world but knows not his own.'[6] He expected that his audience would giggle at this and it did.

Douglas Hyde took his distinguished recruit aside and informed him that there was no need to kidnap an unsuspecting nurse on Aran, as there were many excellent speakers of Irish in the neighbourhood surrounding his nephews' home at Moore Hall. Apparently, this public announcement came as a great surprise to the nephews, who had heard nothing of their uncle's plans. Five months elapsed before their mother was to receive a letter from Ely Place asking her to 'enquire about the woman who speaks the best Irish and engage her to speak Irish all day to the children'.[7] The hapless nephews were not amused to find their days consumed by an Irish-speaking nurse who rattled off sentences, not a word of which they could understand. Not surprisingly, they revolted and the nurse was despatched. Moore was not beaten, however, and at his next public appearance he threatened to disinherit

the children unless they attained fluency in the language
within a single year. Having failed in his appeal to the idealism
of the younger generation, he now tried outrage and threat.
In a final outburst to their recalcitrant mother he wrote: 'It
must be clear to you now that the first thing that concerns
your children is to learn Irish, that whether the nurses are
dirty or ill-mannered is of no moment whatever.'[8] When the
appeal went unanswered, he duly carried out his threat.

Mrs. Maurice Moore was just one of a number of women
who were subjected to Moore's inveterate crusading. He
outraged Lady Gregory at this time with his threat to have
Yeats's *The Shadowy Waters* played in Irish during the third
and final session of the Irish Literary Theatre in 1901. She
insisted on its being acted in English and recorded this shrewd
analysis of Moore in her diary:

> I believe that what gives him his force is his power of
> seeing one thing at a time; at the moment he only sees
> the language, whereas I see the Theatre is the work in
> hand and our immediate duty. *Shadowy Waters* in Irish!
> It would appear to the audience as *Three Men in a Boat*
> talking gibberish![9]

This diagnosis of the brevity and fury of Moore's devotions
bears a suspicious resemblance to that offered by Max
Beerbohm earlier that year in the *Saturday Review*:

> It is one of Mr. Moore's peculiarities that whatever is
> uppermost in his mind seems to him to be the one thing
> in the world, and he cannot conceive that there will
> ever be room for anything else... But if the Keltic
> Renascence prove to be the most important movement
> ever made in Art, it will not long enchain him.[10]

For the time being, however, Moore's enthusiasm only
gathered fire. Despite the strictures of Lady Gregory, he knew
that both the theatre and the Gaelic League had much to
gain from a diplomatic alliance. The theatre could recruit
actors and stage-hands from the ranks of the League, while
the language movement would find in the stage the ideal

platform for its gospel. In the *New Ireland Review* Moore
wrote in April 1900: 'The performance of plays in our
language is part and parcel of the Irish Literary Theatre,
which was founded to create a new centre for Irish enthusiasm, a new outlet for national spirit and energy. This is
the first object of the Irish Literary Theatre; I may say it
is its only object, for if we achieve this we achieve every
object.'[11] He then announced that they planned to produce
The Land of Heart's Desire by Yeats in an Irish translation
prepared by Douglas Hyde. Clearly, Lady Gregory had won
her point. Defending his choice of a translation for the first
production of a Gaelic play, Moore pointed to the difficulties
of acquiring the craft of writing for the stage and to the
limited number of writers in Irish. He emphasised the potentially drastic long-term effects on Gaelic drama of producing
a bad play in the language, while cheerfully conceding that
at this early stage in the progress of the Gaelic League, 'there
will be few in the theatre who will understand an Irish
play.'

This article came to a climax with a warning that the
native language, 'in which resides the soul of the Irish people',
was 'slipping into the grave'. He called for 'a great national
effort to save it'.[12] Answering the stock objections that Irish
literature was merely a formless folklore and an improper
medium for art, Moore argued that the words of Ibsen, written
in a language used by only a few million people, were known
all over Europe. Furthermore, the glories of ancient Irish
literature were celebrated by scholars from all parts of the
world. It was the English rather than the Irish language which
was unsuitable for artistic production. 'From universal use
and journalism, the English language in fifty years will be as
corrupt as the Latin of the eighth century, as unfit for literary
usage, and will become, in my opinion, a sort of Volapuk,
strictly limited to commercial letters and journalism.'[13] He
recalled how he had been struck by the refined beauty of
some passages translated from the Irish writings of an islander,
but that the English written by the same person was coarse
and ugly. 'In either case the writer wrote artlessly, without
selection, but in one case he was using a language in which all
expressions are true and appropriate, and in the other case he

was writing in a language defiled by too long usage.'[14] His
belief was that the future of poetry lay with the languages of
national minorities, Irish, Flemish, Hungarian, Welsh and
Basque. When this article was published with minor alterations one year later in *Ideals in Ireland* (1901), he outlined
his policies even more clearly, offering a partial retraction of
his earlier statement that there would be few to understand
an Irish play. An addendum to page 45 now read: 'Mr. George
Moore wishes to add that at the time he wrote this passage he
did not know of the extraordinary revival of the Irish language
in Dublin.' Lady Gregory, who was the editor of *Ideals in
Ireland*, considered this sentence sufficiently important to
have it printed in red ink on a specially inserted page in the
collection. However, the most important addition to the
earlier article was Moore's blunt declaration of his position:
'Our desire is to make Ireland a bilingual country — to use
English as a universal tongue, and to save our own as a
medium for some future literature.'[15]

Moore's belief in the theatre as an important, but secondary, weapon of the language movement was calculated to
recommend him to the Gaelic League. Its leader, Douglas
Hyde, had declared himself 'convinced of the importance of
using the stage to promote the revival of the native Irish
language as a medium of literature'.[16] In an interview with
the *Freeman's Journal* in 1901 Moore agreed that 'the central
idea of the Theatre would be the restoration of the Irish
language'.[17] In the same year Frank Fay expressed his hope
for actors who would be native speakers, but he was realistic
enough to admit his fear that 'we shall not be so lucky as to
get people of this sort'.[18] Within twelve months Fay had
settled for a national theatre in English, to the great dismay
of Moore who would have preferred to see him touring the
provinces with a group of Gaelic players. The closing months
of 1901 were filled with preparations by Yeats and Moore for
the production of the play *Diarmuid and Grania*, to be per-
formed in conjunction with Hyde's one-act drama, *Casadh an
tSúgáin*. Despite his genuine enthusiasm for the English work,
Moore could not help treating that part of the project with
some flippancy, as when he suggested a master plan to purify
the idiom of the noble characters — he would compose the

play in French, Lady Gregory would translate it into English, Tadhg Ó Donnchadha ('Tórna') would then render it in Irish, and finally Lady Gregory would remould that version in English. The result of these perverse manoeuvres was greeted with some disdain by the nationalist press. The drama critic of *The Leader* unleashed a diatribe against the authors: 'Mr. Yeats and Mr. Moore have twisted the Gaelic story beyond recognition and have changed Diarmuid from a Fenian chief into a modern degenerate.'[19] But Moore couldn't have cared less, for he was in full agreement with the editor of *The Leader* that 'the chief use of Irish drama at present is to popularize the use of the Irish language'.[20] All through the rehearsals, he had stressed that point in conversations with Yeats which are recalled in *Salve*: 'But our play doesn't matter, Yeats; what matters is *The Twisting of the Rope*. We either want to make Irish the language of Ireland, or we don't; and if we do, nothing else matters' (*Hail and Farewell*, p. 315). Though Yeats could never assent for long to such patriotic rather than artistic priorities, there were occasions when he demonstrated a willingness to condone Moore's way of thinking. For example, at the famous luncheon party at which Moore threatened to disinherit his nephews, Yeats had pleased Hyde with the statement that 'the vital question of the moment was the Irish language question', and that it was their own misfortune that the literary society had had to work in the English language.[21]

Moore's commitment to the Gaelic League reached a climax in the first issue of *Samhain*, the journal of the Irish Literary Theatre, where he introduced *Casadh an tSúgáin* in October 1901:

In a way, it would have pleased our vanity to have been the first in Dublin with an Irish play, but this would have been a base vanity and unworthy of a Gaelic Leaguer. There has been no more disinterested movement than the Gaelic League. It has worked for the sake of the langugage without hope of reward or praise; if I were asked why I put my faith in the movement I would answer that to believe that a movement distinguished by so much sacrifice could fail would be like believing in the failure of goodness itself.[22]

In the same year, he continued to bombard the press with interviews and articles in defence of the language, remarking in 'A Plea for the Soul of the Irish People' that 'in five years it has become an honour to know the language which in my youth was considered a disgrace'.[23] Addressing himself to his many readers in England, he declared that the death of a language was 'an act of iconoclasm more terrible than the bombardment of the Parthenon'.[24] In return for the lost Gaelic legends and the open fields of Connemara, the English could offer only 'the gutter press of London' and 'the universal suburb, in which a lean man with glasses on his nose and a black bag in his hand is always running after the bus'.[25] Londoners were suitably insulted, but the Gaelic League was not particularly impressed. The very stridency of Moore's language caused suspicion and amusement — and there were even some ignoble souls who suggested that this stridency arose not from Moore's desire to convince others but from his incapacity to convince himself. When Moore called on the little office of the Gaelic League in Dublin, he was dismayed to find that his name was unknown to the secretary and compensated for his lost dignity by muttering 'seamstresses, seamstresses' under his breath.

However, he had devised a master plan to bring himself to the notice of the Leaguers: the preparation of a collection of short stories for translation into Irish. By its very title *The Untilled Field* proclaimed itself an example to future Gaelic authors of the kind of work to be done. Accordingly, it was first published in an Irish version in 1902 as *An tÚr-Ghort*. Moore later described it as 'a book written in the beginning out of no desire for self-expression but in the hope of furnishing the young Irish of the future with models'.[26] It became a great deal more than a literary model, however, developing into a study of clerical oppression and written in a corrosively realistic style. Moore was overjoyed to see the Irish version of his name 'Seorsa Ó Mórdha' on the book's cover, which also featured the name of Pádraig Ó Súilleabhain of Trinity College, who translated all but one of the stories. The remaining story, 'An Gúna-Phósta' ('The Wedding Gown') had been translated by Tadhg Ó Donnchadha in a version that particularly pleased Moore. When he got T.W. Rolleston to translate 'An Gúna-Phosta' back into English, Moore was entranced with his own lines, finding them 'much improved after their bath in Irish'. He gave as an example 'She had a face such as one sees in a fox', which he deemed far superior to his own flaccid 'She had a fox-like face'. He compared this revitalized phrase to 'a jaded townsman refreshed by a dip in the primal sea'.[27] However, scarcely a hundred copies of *An tÚr-Ghort* were sold and the author never achieved his ambition of seeing the volume displayed in the Gaelic League window. The only real benefit he derived from the experience was the assistance of Rolleston's versions of the Gaelic as he made final preparations for the publication of *The Untilled Field* in the following year. He continued, though, to assert the importance of providing Gaelic writers with the best models and constantly nagged Hyde with suggestions for translating various English and Continental classics into Irish.[28]

His finest hour was yet to come. At the start of 1902 he went into conclave with Hyde, in order to lay plans for that contradiction in terms, a Gaelic lawn party. He wrote in a state of high excitement to his brother, Colonel Maurice Moore:

> I want to give a party. The garden in front of my house belongs to me and it will hold five or six hundred people easily; and there are apple trees; and nothing will be easier than to build a stage. . . On this stage I want to have performed a play in Irish. I want to have a Gaelic-speaking audience. I think this would be a very good thing, and I think it would annoy Dublin society very much, which will add considerably to my pleasure.[29]

Soon Hyde's play *An Tincéar agus an tSídheog* (*The Tinker and the Fairy*) went into rehearsal with the actors all drawn from the Gaelic League, including the author himself and Sinéad Ní Fhlannagáin (later to become Mrs. Éamon de Valera). Moore treated the actors who trooped through his house during rehearsals with the most exquisite tact, but when the great day dawned he seemed at a complete loss, for

he had never before given a party. 'What am I do to?' he asked
the Leaguers, and in the event decided simply to do nothing
other than beam beatifically at all of the guests. They must
have been a motley collection of people, those shopgirls and
office clerks mingling in Ely Place with professors and
portrait painters, under the disapproving gaze of Moore's
neighbours who looked down in derision from their high
windows. Or so John Butler Yeats thought, as he recalled the
strange event in a letter to his daughter Lily:

> There was a great crowd there. Tyrrell, F.T.C.D. was the
> only F.T.C.D. there... The weather held up alright at
> the play. There had been a bitter, black storm of rain in
> the morning, but it cleared up... The play ought to
> have started at 3 o'clock when the sun was shining and
> it was quite warm, and that was the time appointed. But
> the delegates (I don't know what delegates) did not
> arrive. Meanwhile, the sky began to blacken and we all
> felt anxious while Moore, in his peculiar manner, kept
> softly gesticulating his despair. At last, the wretches
> arrived and the play began, and though expecting every
> moment to be drenched through, we got safely to the
> end; though for a time all umbrellas were up, which
> might have been pleasant for the people trying to see.
> Fortunately, this happened towards the end, when the
> musicians and singers (out of sight behind a screen of
> leaves) had the performance to themselves.[30]

As Moore waved farewell to Hyde later that afternoon, he
must already have been studying the shape of the gentle
scholar's head in search of an appropriate satirical phrase. By
the time Moore had embarked on his autobiography, Hyde
had been transformed from a genial scholar in a suburban
garden to the abject butt of his most lethal lines. 'Nothing
libels a man so much as his own profile', wrote Moore. 'Hyde
looked like an imitation Irish speaker; in other words, like a
stage Irishman' (*Hail and Farewell*, p. 139). He recalled 'the
droop of the moustache through which his Irish frothed like
porter, and when he returned to English it was easy to understand why he desired to change the language of Ireland'

(p. 238). Why this sudden contempt? An answer may be found in Moore's growing anticlericalism. He was greatly irritated by the way in which Hyde curried favour with all sections of the rising Catholic bourgeoisie, 'members of Parliament, priests, farmers, shopkeepers'. 'By standing well with these people, especially with the priests,' complained Moore, 'he had become the archtype of the Catholic-Protestant, cunning, subtle, cajoling, superficial and affable.' By such devices Hyde had managed 'to paddle the old dug-out of the Gaelic League up from the marshes'. For Moore, just then engaged in an announcement of his defection to Protestantism in *The Irish Times*, such abject deference by a distinguished Protestant to the Catholic clergy was lamentable. So he poured scorn on the man whose work he had once compared with that of Homer.

Already the Catholic clergy were taking control of entire branches of the League, to the dismay not only of Moore but of the young James Joyce. In his early novel *Stephen Hero*, Joyce acidly noted that 'the meetings of Friday nights were public and were largely patronised by priests'.[31] Joyce's own view of the League emerges in a conversation between Stephen and the enthusiast Madden. Stephen considers the Roman, not the Sassenach, to be the real tyrant of the island. He suggests that the belated support for the dying language was given by a clergy which considered it a safeguard for their flock against the wolves of disbelief, 'an opportunity to withdraw their people into a past of literal, implicit faith'. Moore would have heartily agreed. He had made the cynical observation that 'the Roman Catholic church relies upon its converts, for after two or three generations of Catholicism the intelligence dies' (*Hail and Farewell*, p. 434). His study of translations of early Gaelic literature had vindicated Yeats's belief that it was heathily bereft of abstract ideas; but the pathetic inadequacy of later Gaelic art demonstrated, he felt, just how corrosive was the effect of Catholic teaching on the artistic intelligence. 'The only time Ireland had a literature was when she had no ideas — in the eighth and ninth centuries' commented Moore (p. 344). 'As soon as the Irish Church became united to Rome, art declined in Ireland. . . Irish Catholics have written very little. . . After a hundred years of education it (Maynooth) has not succeeded in producing a book of any value' (pp. 352-3). Now that the products of Maynooth were beginning to appear on Hyde's platforms, Moore began to look upon them with a very jaundiced eye. In *Ave* he offered the same analysis as Joyce:

> . . . a young cleric said that he was in favour of a revival of the Irish language because no heresy had ever been written in it. A fine reason it was to give why we should be at pains to revive the language, and it had awakened a suspicion in me that he was just a lad — in favour of the Irish language because there was no thought in its literature. What interest is there in any language but for the literature it has produced or is going to produce? (p. 241)

Moore had returned to Ireland in the belief that the Gaelic League would waken the land from the great sleep of Catholicism; but now, under the indulgent eye of Hyde and his clerical cohorts, Ireland was slumbering more peacefully than ever.

Of course, Moore had suspected as much all along. Hence the covert irony and self-mocking extravagance of his more extreme pro-Gaelic statements. Even the description of the *Daily Express* dinner for the Irish Literary Theatre is shot through with the misgivings which had haunted the new recruit as he mounted the platform of dignitaries and listened in consternation to the sounds of his native tongue:

> It seems to be a language suitable for the celebration of an antique Celtic rite, but too remote for modern use. It had never been spoken by ladies in silken gowns with fans in their hands or by gentlemen going out to kill each other with engraved rapiers or pistols. Men had merely cudgelled each other, yelling strange oaths the while in Irish, and I remembered it in the mouths of the old fellows dressed in breeches and worsted stockings, swallowtail coats and tall hats full of dirty bank-notes, which they used to give my father. Since those days I had not heard Irish, and when Hyde began to speak it

an instinctive repulsion rose up in me, quelled with
difficulty, for I was already a Gaelic Leaguer. (p. 139)

The repulsion is *instinctive*. Subsequent experience was
simply to increase Moore's misgivings; and even the model for
a future Gaelic literature, *An tÚr-Ghort*, is filled with that
same repulsion, as if the author's unconfessed mission was to
have that repulsion expressed for the first time in his native
language. Distaste for the language all too easily became distaste for the entire country. So Ned Carmady in 'The Wild
Goose' opts for emigration in the belief that it is better to die
than to live in Ireland, a maxim curiously prophetic of
Beckett's avowal that he preferred to live in France at war
than in Ireland at peace. The hero of 'In the Clay' makes a
similar observation: '(Ireland) is no country for an educated
man.'[32]

It was, perhaps, the failure of the Gaelic League to respond
to the challenge posed by *An tÚr-Ghort* which — more than
anything else — convinced Moore that its writers would never
create a major literature. He could have endured praise or
enjoyed abuse, but he had no use for apathy. Even if (as
Patrick Pearse repeatedly stressed) the language could be a
realistic medium for a modern writer, Moore estimated that it
would take him ten years to acquire an adequate knowledge
of it, a more charitable span than that which he had allotted
to his disinherited nephews. 'But ten years among the fisher-
folk might blot out all desire of literature in me.' The only
remaining hope was that a native Aran Islander, endowed
with literary genius, might put pen to paper, 'but the possibility
of genius, completely equipped, arising in the Arran Islands
seemed a little remote' (*Hail and Farewell*, p. 75). It was
more than twenty years later that Liam O'Flaherty began to
make his name, but apart from some skilful short stories by
Pádraig Ó Conaire and Patrick Pearse, there was no revival of
Gaelic literature while Moore sojourned at Ely Place. By
1908 he could write to Edouard Dujardin that 'the Celtic
Renascence does not exist — it is a myth, like a good many
other things'.[33] Nevertheless, he was modest enough to aver
before his English audience that if he had managed to learn
Irish and write in it, the language would now be 'a flourishing

concern' (*Hail and Farewell*, p. 74).

In his autobiography Moore chose to treat his brief career as a Gaelic revivalist with a dismissive and insolent flippancy. This led most critics to assume that the entire affair was from the very outset an elaborate joke at the expense of literary Dublin. Moore connived in this interpretation by suggesting that his public speeches and articles were pure fabrications, 'merely intellectual, invented so that the Gaelic League should be able to justify its existence with reasonable, literary argument' (p. 235). But it would be wrong to assume that the corrosive tone of *Hail and Farewell* had also characterised his relations with the Gaelic League and the Literary Theatre. The insolent satire which permeates that brilliant but wilful book tells us a great deal about Moore's state of mind between 1910 and 1914, but reveals nothing of the passionate intensity with which he threw himself into the work of the Gaelic League in 1901 and 1902. Those who knew him well in his Dublin years — men like John Eglinton and George Russell — were in no doubt as to the depth of his commitment, which they found at times ridiculous, but which he himself learned to mock only when it had abated. At the time of his passion he was perfectly capable of expressing grave doubts about the authenticity of George Russell's visions, on the grounds that the mystic poet did not know the Irish language and could not therefore expect to converse with the Celtic gods. If there is a note of scornful irony in the pages of *Hail and Farewell* then that scorn is directed not so much at the idealists of the Gaelic League as at the intensity of the author's earlier devotion.

For all his subsequent disclaimers, Moore's flirtation with the Gaelic movement proved surprisingly influential. His dream of translating the classics of England and the Continent into Irish was finally realised with the foundation of An Gúm in 1926, the government-sponsored press which employed such fine writers as Máirtín Ó Cadhain and Seosamh Mac Grianna to do just that. Furthermore, Moore's disenchantment with the corrupting effects of journalism was shared by many contemporaries, including Yeats, who later went on to blame 'a violent contemporary paper' and 'a patriotic journalism' for the attacks on Abbey art.[34] The theory that English had become worn from over-use became a subject of impassioned debate in the ensuing decade. Yeats endorsed the ideas of Moore, while Russell insisted that words can never be utterly debased by anyone, that even the threadbare idioms of the journalist can be revitalised by an artist of vision and emotion. It was left to Synge to reconcile these conflicting theories. He conceded Moore's point that words have a cycle of life, but insisted that the time came when they were too exhausted, even for the journalist. At such a time, they might be restored to their original power, in line with Emerson's belief that 'every word was once a poem'.

It was, however, the policy of selective bilingualism which proved the most durable of Moore's legacies, for it is that ideal which still dominates the debate on the future of the Irish language. Moore saw English as the language of business, journalism and commerce with the outside world, Irish as the idiom of culture, education and the domestic life. In many respects his ideas remarkably anticipate the more sophisticated concept of *diglossia* expounded by Máirtin Ó Murchú in his study *Language and Community* (1970). *Diglossia* is defined as the societal patterning of two codes in sets of situations, usually exclusive, where the use of each code is clearly defined by social convention. As a concrete example of this, Ó Murchú cites the normal division of Arabic into a set of domains where a high subcode is used (church sermons, university lectures, news broadcasts), and an informal set of domains where a low subcode is used (instruction to servants, domestic conversation, captions in political cartoons). Moore would have been in profound agreement with the immediate goal of 'an Irish-English *diglossia* along such lines, in which Irish would have a significant part to play consistent with its function as the national language'.[35]

For good or for ill, the ideas of George Moore still prove a fertile source of discussion among writers and scholars, over sixty years after he himself abandoned them. The ripples of appreciation and amusement which emanated from his quaint garden party at Ely Place have never quite died.

MOORE'S WAY BACK: *THE UNTILLED FIELD* AND *THE LAKE*

Robert Welch

I

Those who have written of George Moore's part in the Irish literary revival have recognised the significance, for the man and for his art, of his return to Ireland in 1901. He was tired of England, and wanted to play a part in the rejuvenation of life he felt was starting to take place in Ireland.

Moore had been living and working as a man of letters in London since his father's death in 1880, and had made a name for himself as the English exponent of the naturalism of Zola and the impassioned realism of Balzac. By the time he left England he had developed two major pre-occupations as a writer: first, he placed great value on the individual gaining, through experience and self-scrutiny, some insight into and acceptance of his own nature; and secondly, he felt that happiness was something to be realized through achieving an interplay with the inevitable unpredictability of life. That mind is wisest and happiest, he would say, when it is self-possessed enough to be flexibly engaged with what, simply, happens. This was a quality he found mostly in women, which is why he liked them so much, wrote so well of them, and distrusted the abstracted melancholy male rigidities can create. Alice Barton in *A Drama in Muslin*, and Esther Waters in the novel of that title are both embodiments of a wise feminine compliance to life's dictates.

Towards the end of the 1890s Moore thought that England was becoming drearily masculine, rigid, and inflexible. The Boer War he saw as evidence of a new imperialist materialism. In *Ave* he describes how he could see the greed for the gold fields in Pretoria disfiguring the faces of anonymous people in Piccadilly: 'everybody's bearing and appearance suggested to me a repugnant sensual cosmopolitanism'.[1]

The English landscape darkened on him; English poetry, his beloved Shelley's *Prometheus Unbound* even, failed to rouse him out of his disaffection. He became annoyed by the verbal system of the language itself, thinking that English verbs had lost all their charge. He described it as: 'a woolly language without a verbal system or agreement between the adjectives and nouns' (p. 223).

All of this, needless to say, tells us more about Moore's state of mind at the time than it does about England or the English language. We recognise, as Moore himself did later (his moods of these years are ironically replayed in *Hail and Farewell*), the inane simplifications of hysteria. Not surprisingly, given this attitude, and the fact that at the time he was engaged in trying to guide Yeats out of the Fomorian tangle he had got himself into in writing *The Shadowy Waters*, one day Cathleen ni Houlihan herself put in an appearance while he was gazing at the Burren, during a visit to Ireland. 'A sentimental craving for the country itself', was what he called the emotion that this experience aroused in him, 'a certain pity, at variance with my character, that had seemed to rise out of my heart' (p. 208). He is describing, not without embarrassment, a sense of *personal* relationship with the country that many Irishmen have felt and still feel. It is not republican, it is not necessarily patriotic, and it will not do to label it Romantic transcendentalism. It is, however, often conveniently defined negatively, by establishing England as an opposite to be hated, a mechanical male brutality rummaging Ireland's feminine compliance, and this is the disturbing process that Moore chronicles for us in *Hail and Farewell*. He had become susceptible.

Life darkened for him, and he found himself in a situation, appalling for a realist, where his moods no longer easily engaged with the inevitable patterns of daily life. It was a time of psychological and artistic crisis and it was evidently a very disturbing thing for him to hear, on the Hospital Road in Chelsea, a voice coming, not from within, but without, urging him to 'go to Ireland' (p. 257). However one chooses to regard this (and though Moore makes fun of the whole thing in the aloof irony of *Hail and Farewell*, it is far from certain that this was his attitude at the time), there is no doubt that in returning to Ireland he was following an inscrutable impulse from his own unconscious. This, of course, is what Oliver Gogarty does in *The Lake* when he *leaves* Ireland.

There were other reasons, too, more amenable to rational evaluation, for his return to Ireland: he was, with Edward Martyn and W.B. Yeats, a director of the Irish Literary Theatre; he had become convinced of the desirability of reviving the Irish language, and had written and spoken on behalf of the Gaelic League (even threatening to disinherit his brother Maurice's children if they were not brought up in Irish); he was enthralled by Yeats's transcendental idealism, so much at odds with the plain sobriety of the Saxon, which now bored, where it once reassured. But in the end, he was following his instincts. He had reached a turning point, a crisis, of which his estrangement from England and his eccentric attitude towards the education of his brother's children were symptoms. His life had gone dead on him, psychologically and artistically, and the way out was to leave, to go into exile from his dead life and make a new life for himself in the old place.

II

The Irish language, which, he wrote to his brother, 'interests me more than anything else', seemed to incorporate, in what he knew, in theory, of its concreteness and lack of abstraction, its energy and activity, this new life.[2] Though he was, he thought, too old to learn the language, he formed the idea of assisting the Gaelic Revival by writing stories of Irish life, to be translated into Irish by Taidgh O'Donoghue (Moore's spelling) for publication in the Jesuit periodical, the *New Ireland Review*, which was edited by Fr. Tom Finlay. The idea was that Fr. Tom would get a collection of these stories accepted as a text book for the Intermediate Board of Education

(*Hail and Farewell* p. 343). Three of the stories appeared in the journal — the Irish versions of 'The Wedding Gown' ('An Gúna Phósta'), 'Almsgiving' ('An Déirc'), and 'The Clerk's Quest' ('Tóir Mhic Uí Dhíomasuigh') — but the editor felt that the subsequent stories, 'Homesickness' and 'The Exile', could hardly be included in a textbook for schools, mainly because of the increasing bitterness of Moore's attacks on the Irish Catholic clergy.

After a lengthy engagement with late nineteenth century English Catholicism in *Evelyn Innes* (1898) and *Sister Teresa* (1901), Moore, almost as soon as he returned to Ireland, began to formulate the idea that the cultural and emotional stagnation that he found there were attributable to the rigid mindlessness of its clerical institutions. Where he had imagined Ireland a domain of spiritual freshness and vivid life he began to see it as a place petrified by a pious anxiety to keep life orderly and respectable. The priests, in Moore's view, went in for an abstract transcendentalism shored up by platitude and prejudice, which denied the changeableness that he saw as life's very essence.

Art, Moore would argue, remains faithful to the changing quality of life's patterns; it does not simplify, console, or dictate. As he wrote these Irish stories he began to re-discover for himself the flexibility of the artist. Like the priests that became the object of his ridicule in 'The Exile' or 'Some Parishioners', he had, on leaving England, been guilty of a kind of inflexibility, the inflexibility of a man with a cause. Now he was beginning to see Ireland as it was, through his writing, which meant detaching himself from those simplicities he had created out of his own emotional need about Ireland in England. Again, the writing involved a departure from a dead view of life into a fuller, because more lively, version of the way things were. He was going into exile from a false self into a realization of a truer one. Exile, thought of in this way, may be the only real condition for a writer to be in (as Joyce too discovered): it means forsaking the old moulds assumed out of duty, obligation, hysteria or exhaustion, to accommodate the self to the new shapes life is continually evolving; it is realism deepening to wisdom.

Why, it might be asked, is Moore, in *The Untilled Field*

and *The Lake*, so interested in the priests of a church which he regards as a stranglehold on the spontaneity of life in Ireland? One of the reasons, surely, why he can write so well of them, why the play of irony often sharpens into anger, is that he himself knew only too well the attraction, for a mind not self-possessed, of a code of fixed ideas, a cause. There was in Moore (as in Joyce) a good deal of the priest. He wrote well of the comforts of the presbytery, the beeswaxed security of the convent, but he also showed, in the writing he did in Ireland (and subsequently), that life's impulses are constantly escaping (going into exile from) the constraints orthodoxy would place upon them. This makes him, as a writer, capable of celebration.

Characteristically, the celebration is often tempered by the sense that the freedom obtained by throwing off the old ways can be a bleak freedom. It is so for Catherine in 'The Exile', who leaves the comfort of the convent for the difficult 'loneliness' of the outside world: she marries a man whom she loves but who doesn't particularly care for her, and who is something of an ineffectual. Much the finest man in the story is her husband's brother, James, who is in love with her, and because he is goes to America, leaving the farm for the couple. There is no simple message here; the story presents the complex difficulties of life's choices with objectivity and sympathy.

However, Moore does not develop an interior life for James which would allow us to see his decision to leave for America as an inevitable progression of his nature: it is an abrupt story, but also delicate, in that it does not belie the way life transforms one set of situations into another.

There are other stories in *The Untilled Field* which explore, in greater depth, the transitions life brings about in a character's ideas about himself or about others, — Bryden in 'Homesickness' for example.

Kate Kavanagh, too, in 'The Wedding Feast', gets out, to America, away from her arranged marriage to Peter MacShane. She knows 'there's no judging for oneself'[3] in Ireland, and opts to go with the unpredictability of her own nature, her own odd, aloof freedom, which can, on the morning of crisis, after she has kept her husband of a few hours out of her bedroom, allow her to think that elderflower water is good for the complexion.

Moore, then, returned to Ireland with fixed ideas and a certain amount of idealized illusion about the country, the language, and the people.

To begin with, the stories of *The Untilled Field* were written for the cause, but gradually, as his understanding of Ireland and his relationship with it complicated, the writing became a form of departure, a kind of exile, from those fixed ideas and illusions. It became a mode of exploring the shifting unpredictability of life, its constant susceptibility to change, and in so doing the writing itself grew more accurate, freer, in that it too drew closer to the way things are, thereby acquiring a better, because more humane and flexible, quality of judging.

The story 'Almsgiving', though it does not have Ireland or the clergy for its theme, is all about the change from a set of false ideas to a fuller engagement with the way things are. At the beginning, the narrator meets a blind beggar in a dark passageway, and searches his voluminous clothing for a penny, but the rain coming on he walks quickly away. The narrator is oppressed by the thought of the bleak life of the beggar, and he imagines how much fuller it would be if he had the companionship of a dog. From then on the narrator avoids the blind man's dark place, until one day, on an impulse, he goes back. They talk, and to his amazement, he finds that the object of his sentimental pity has a family, that the children go on holidays to the seaside, and that the blind man himself has a friend, a policeman, who takes him out for the odd day. The story concludes:

> A soft south wind was blowing, and an instinct as soft and gentle filled my heart, and I went towards some trees. The new leaves were beginning in the high branches. I was sitting where sparrows were building their nests, and very soon I seemed to see farther into life than I had ever seen before. 'We're here,' I said, 'for the purpose of learning what life is, and the blind beggar has taught me a great deal, something that I could not have learnt out of a book, a deeper truth than any book

contains . . .'. And then I ceased to think, for thinking is a folly when a soft south wind is blowing and an instinct as soft and gentle fills the heart. (pp. 199-200)

There is a Joycean quality in these cadences, in the soft repetitions, but also in the quality of the insight, of which the style is the epiphanic expression. There is a gaucheness there as well: all this talk of learning and teaching is a bit heavy-handed, but it in no way invalidates the depth the writing sounds. Moore is celebrating the re-awakening to life out of the deathly rigour of prejudice and opinion. The narrator thinks the blind man's life a dismal thing, lived out in a dark place, but in the end it is he who receives alms: the gift of comprehension of the beggar's life, its variety and richness. The shallowness of the earlier, neurotic reaction is contrasted with the humanity of the later. The narrator divests himself of the encumbering comfort of the 'several coats' of prejudice to discover a more complete understanding (p. 194). 'Instinct' is the word Moore has for it here, and it is the awakening of Fr. Gogarty's instinctual life that is to be his main preoccupation in *The Lake*.

III

The story 'In the Clay' opened the first edition of *The Untilled Field*, and this, with 'The Way Back', formed, as John Cronin has shown,[4] a loose framework for the book. Moore dropped these stories from the continental edition of 1903. He reworked them for the 1931 edition as a single story in two parts, called 'Fugitives'.

In neither version is the material handled in a satisfactory way, and yet, as is clear from the publishing history, Moore could not leave it alone. The reason for this, one suspects, is because the stories explore themes and concerns that deeply pre-occupied Moore at the time of writing and before, and that continued to pre-occupy him for the rest of his career: the role the modern creative artist might have in Ireland;

the 'Celtic Renaissance'; the reasons for returning to Ireland; the reasons for exile; the possible relationship between the art of Ireland and that of France or Italy. No wonder he never quite mastered the material out of which these stories are drawn: he had to wait for the cool eccentric irony of *Hail and Farewell* before he could do that.

These framing stories are about a Dublin sculptor called Rodney, who does work for a Fr. McCabe.[5] McCabe dreams of reviving Celtic Romanesque as an architectural style, and of building a church 'in the line of' Cormac's chapel at Cashel. His sculptor, Rodney, is also ineffectual. He dreams that in another time he might have been an apprentice to Benvenuto Cellini. His one exceptional piece of work is a clay figure for a virgin and child which he has modelled from the nude. The girl who sat for him, Lucy Delaney, he saw in a solicitor's office, and he admired her 'long tapering legs and sinuous back'. His intention is to cover up the nude with the appropriate pious drapery after he has it cast as a classic piece, but he makes the mistake of showing the clay figure to McCabe, who, it turns out, is related to the girl who sat for him. McCabe is scandalized, and he tells Lucy's fat father about her sittings. The father starts shouting, and Lucy's younger brothers overhear the row. Not understanding the full story they decide to go around to Rodney's studio that night to have a look at the statue that is causing all the fuss. By accident they knock it over and shatter it. Rodney leaves Ireland in disgust and meets the Irish novelist, Harding, in London. Harding has become converted to the cause of the Irish Renaissance, and is on his way back to Ireland, but Rodney is off, defiantly, to the blue sunlit shadows of Frascati and the narrow streets of Perugia. Harding, it turns out, has met Lucy in London and been tempted to seduce her, but she has gone to America to marry a mathematical instrument maker in Chicago called Wainscott. (Moore's names for his characters are often peculiar.)

The nude figure of Lucy is the best thing Rodney has done, the closest he has come to creating something free of the encumbrances of convention, mediocrity, seeing at second-hand. Here was an art attentive to the pliant sinuousness, the supple freedom and excitement, of a real woman's body. It was from the life. He had freed himself from the dreary piousness of McCabe's commission, only to have his one true piece of work broken by a stupid accident caused by the priest's frightened outrage at that freedom. So, he goes into exile.

But Rodney is far from the tragic artist, isolated among the ignorant. He is a mediocre man himself. Apart from his failure to insist on his own vision until his last Irish commission, he remains guilty of a human failure in his attitude to Lucy. He cannot respond to her need to break out of the dreary predictability of her own life; he remains remote from her, untouched by the life his art has begun to celebrate. He is a bit of a prig. So that, while Moore writes with understanding of his dilemma, he also makes him effete and superficial. Rodney is enthusiastic about Italy, but the suspicion lurks that his exile there may only be a superficial thing: the blue shadows of the Mediterranean afternoons may be no more to him than were Lucy's legs, a kind of aesthetic titillation with no real engagement, no searching out of the self, through contact with a life outside it.

Indeed voyeurism is a minor theme of these two framing stories: when Harding met Lucy his first thought was how he might take advantage of her. When he tells Rodney of what happened between them, the sculptor correctly diagnoses the mood of sexual possibility that Harding was excited by when he compares her to a pot of jam that the novelist might put away for private delectation:

> 'Like a pot of jam left carefully under cover. How well I can see you going away saying: "that will be all right till tomorrow"'. (p. 335)

'Very likely', is Harding's response to this suggestion. It gets worse. Harding tells how he got out a photograph of women bathing (to get him into the mood, one supposes) and how he thought of reviving a long dormant interest in painting in order that she might pose for him as she did for his friend. She refuses, but it is all a bit prurient. He does right by her in the end, but it is partly through fear of being discovered.

This then is Harding's encounter with Lucy, briefly sket-

ched, so that, when he declares himself a convert to the Irish
Renaissance the reader is already schooled in his unreliability,
opportunism, and inner faithlessness, the kind of qualities,
Moore would seem to be suggesting, that make one eager for
the cold comfort of fixed ideas and the rigidity of a dead life,
whether it be that which the garb of clerical office imposes,
or that other, not less mortifying kind, that cultural nationalism would insist upon.

These two artists, Rodney and Harding, are, to some extent,
superficial men, who have not, in the phrase of Saul Bellow's
Henderson, taken their lives to a certain depth. They have not
worked down into a sensed comprehension of their interior
selves and all that that involves: their instincts (to use Moore's
word from 'Almsgiving'), their conscious and unconscious
motives, their feelings about Ireland, are unknown to them.
Their inner lives are an 'untilled field'.

In framing the collecting with these two stories (later con-
flated into one), Moore is laying his cards on the table, but in
a curiously oblique way. The stories are not satisfactory in
that the hidden lives of the characters remain a mystery to
them, and to us, but in a way this is precisely the effect that
Moore is after. They depict the untilled field of the Irish
consciousness, which is the book's theme and the challenge
that it takes on. Moore wants to dig down into a life that
'had never been expressed' (this last phrase, which Yeats
claimed he used to Synge, urging him to go to Aran, reminds
us of how widespread this nationalist and literary ambition
was at the time[6]) and his slightly playful handling of Rodney
and Harding is a kind of ironic exorcism of his creative fear
of failing to do just that. They are slightly silly examples of
what it is he hopes to avoid.

It is, perhaps, something of a negative framework for the
first edition of the book (which must be why he dropped the
stories from the continental edition) but in the final analysis
it is true to his own ambiguous feelings about his commitment, his nervousness on embarking on a subject so close to
him, and about which he himself could, by virtue of a strong
dose of idealistic nationalism (satirized in Harding), become
inflexible, rigid, priestly, McCabe-like.[7]

As he wrote the main body of the book, he worked deeper,

finding access here and there, in no easily consistent way, to the buried lives of the people and the country, whose quality of inner experience he wished to express. But it is only in *The Lake* that he overcomes the difficulty of working down into the 'underlife'[8] of an Irishman in a completely convincing way. Moore's technique of interior narration, and the fluid style he finds for it, knits Gogarty's mind to the landscape around Lough Carra so intrinsically that its changing colours and shifting moods seem an expression of the changing quality of Gogarty's own mind.

Caught in a web of Irish frustration, timidity, remorse and self-hate, Gogarty gradually, and with great difficulty, learns to attend to the changing process of life within him, the fluid wisdom of instinct. By hearkening to that, the 'lake in every man's heart',[9] Gogarty comes into possession of himself for the first time. The untilled field, if you like, slopes down into the lake.

IV

The Untilled Field shows us how complicated Moore's preoccupation with Ireland was, how it seemed a place of great simplicity and naturalness by comparison with England, but how it was also hampered by prejudices and conventions of its own. The great tryanniser over life's natural instincts was the church, the dreary institutionalism of which seemed to inhibit every living nerve from attaining its own intrinsic spontaneity. The only way out was out, over the water, but the danger there was that the exile might leave, only to find himself caught in the webs spun out of his *own* rigidity, his *own* tyranny over his natural self. The mind is good at making traps to catch itself and one of the most effective of these is to imagine an exterior cause as totally responsible for a personal fault.

The Lake, which, Moore said in the preface to the 1921 edition, belonged 'so strictly' with the stories that his memory included them in the same volume, is all about leaving and what it means, or about what it means to come to leave responsibly. It concentrates and deepens the concerns of the short stories. The plot is very simple: Fr. Gogarty, parish priest of Garranard on the shores of Lough Carra, casts out Nora Glynn, the attractive young schoolmistress who has become pregnant, by speaking against her from the altar. He is a Jehovah, a tyranniser, a judger, over her, but over himself as well. A correspondence develops, first with Fr. O'Grady, who looked after Nora when she first came to London, then with Nora herself, during the course of which Gogarty realizes that he has loved her all along and that his incredible public attack on her was powered by his sexual jealousy. He made her the victim of his own affliction. There was a failure of humanity, which, through great distress and illness, he comes to recognise. He realizes that his own life had been a dead one, shored by custom. She, with her individuality, her style, wakened him out of his rigour, but as soon as she did he wanted her for himself and no-one else. Eventually he decides that the only thing for him to do is to make a complete break with his life in Garranard and go to America. At the end of the book he swims the lake, the book's presiding symbol, leaving his clothes by the shore so that his parishioners will presume him drowned.

Moore finds his depth in *The Lake* by making the consciousness of the priest, evolving towards self-knowledge, the central focus of the book. Like the peasants of *The Untilled Field* and like his own parishioners, he belongs to the landscape around him: born and bred there he knows it intimately, even thinking of writing its history. But unlike his parishioners he feels somewhat estranged from it as well; he feels he has got into a rut and needs to change. Moore, in the novel, makes the landscape a constant reflection of his changing thought, his thoughts themselves being as changeable as the differing colours and atmospheres of the lake. The lake is Lough Carra, and Gogarty half-heartedly entertains a scheme to bridge it, but the lake is also the pool of his own instinctual life, his source, which is troubled by his relationship with Nora Glynn. Moore's writing creates a unity between exterior and interior; the style itself is adapted to convey Gogarty's vacillations, the tone of his mind. It is fluid, impressionistic, searching in its meditative syntax. Often he does not know what he thinks, and the style re-enacts that hesitant sensitivity, that doubtful wavering between one thought and another.

An exterior view of Gogarty might have shown him as a randier, more self-conscious McCabe, but through the technical expedient of making the flux of his mind the centre of the novel the intolerance or the slightly comic sympathy Moore tends to have towards the priests in *The Untilled Field* deepens into a more human understanding in *The Lake*. This is why Moore wrote in the 1921 preface that the novel holds a special place in his affections because of the difficulty overcome in the telling:

> the one vital event in the priest's life befell him before the story opens, and to keep the story in the key in which it was conceived, it was necessary to recount the priest's life during the course of his walk by the shores of the lake, weaving his memories continually, without losing sight, however, of the long, winding, mere-like lake, wooded to its shores, with hills appearing and dis-appearing into mist and distance. The difficulty over-come is a joy to the artist, for in his conquest over the material he draws nigh to his idea, and in this book mine was the essential rather than the daily life of the priest, and as I read for this edition, I seemed to hear it. The drama passes within the priest's soul; it is tied and untied by the flux and reflux of sentiments, in-herent in and proper to his nature, and the weaving of a story out of the soul substance without ever seeking the aid of external circumstance seems to me a little triumph. It may be that all ears are not tuned, or are too indifferent or indolent to listen; it is easier to hear 'Esther Waters' and to watch her struggle for her child's life than to hear the mysterious warble, soft as lake water, that abides in the heart. (p. x)

This 'warble' (awkward word) that Moore would have his reader attend to will not imply that he should form an atti-tude for or against Gogarty, or the Ireland out of which he comes. Rather he will see Gogarty's search for the inevitable inclinations of his nature, a quest which is thrust upon him, and which he does not take to gladly or easily, as a search for his own 'soul'. Surely, adds Moore, 'the possession of one's soul is a great reality' (p. 172). Moore would want the reader's assent that a deeper kind of realism is at work in this novel than that more apparent kind which holds his attention in *Esther Waters*.

Gogarty comes into possession of himself by leaving 'the dead wisdom of codes and formulas, dogmas and opinions'. He seeks in the end what he calls a 'vagrancy of ideas and affections' (p. 171), but it is a wise vagrancy, attentive to 'the law of change which is the law of life' (p. 175). The swim across the lake which concludes the novel, beginning with the sheer physical delight of a muscular naked body striving against the dark moonlit water, ending in cold, exhaustion and a touch of fear, is, in its double nature, a fitting coda to this complex novel, which depicts the shifting quality of the human personality in its troubled relations with itself and the world outside it. The lake and the untilled fields about it become an image of that field of complex interaction between the nervous impulses of the mind and the multitudinous world beyond it which it only comes to know with great difficulty. The 'difficulty overcome', to which Moore refers, is the difficulty of getting all this down, and this he did by getting inside his priest, and by finding a style for his 'essential life'. By setting that down he was setting down a portion of the unconscious life of the Ireland of his time, all the more convincing for being somewhat strange and more than a little inconclusive.

V

It is somewhat surprising for us to read, in the 1921 preface, Moore's slightly apologetic comment on *The Lake*: 'I think there will always be a few who will agree with me that there is as much life in *The Lake* as there is in *Esther Waters*.'

His unease about his readers' reactions to the content and technique of *The Lake* may be explained by the fact that in it, in opening fiction up to the shifting uncertainties of consciousness, he was attempting something new in literary narrative. In this, as literary historians point out, he (like Joyce after him) was influenced by his friend Edouard Dujardin's novel *Les Lauriers sont coupés*, and by Wagner's music dramas. Now, of course, Moore's technique has become one of the standard modes of narration in fiction.

His view of the mind, as something constantly changing, has also become fairly standard: Heraclitus, more than any other ancient philosopher, speaks to the mind of our century. But, while in some ways Moore does foreshadow modern relativistic thinking (that sees all things as hopelessly fluid, with nothing clear to be discerned, each man locked in his subjective fall-out shelter, remembering), in other ways he differs. 'The law of change is the law of life' Gogarty says, but while such a law cannot be thought out it can be experienced, by allowing the mind its free play, and the body its instinctual drive. Then, Moore has Gogarty discover, the peculiar and eccentric patterns of his nature clarify themselves, free of the ready made opinions of others: 'there is no moral law except one's own conscience ... the moral obligation of every man is to separate the personal from the impersonal conscience' (p. 173).

The discovery of personal conscience, Gogarty thinks, frees one to love, love being participation, not triumph or tyranny. What Moore celebrates in *The Lake* is the moral flexibility (not indifference) that Gogarty attains through discovering his own spontaneous inner self.

In *Hail and Farewell* Moore's comic vision flows out of a sense of the absurdity of those who, for whatever reason, fail to acknowledge their fluid humanity, their ever changingness. Instead they set up static images of themselves to which they make their behaviour comply. Yeats, for instance, is the magician, the conjuror, the Poet, a mechanical structure sustained (like an umbrella) by the vigour of his belief in himself. If that flags, he collapses. On the other hand the narrative consciousness of the book is totally at ease with its own fluidity and can move backwards and forwards in time at will, questioning itself, finding itself ludicrous, congratulating itself. We are drawn to the voice that weaves and unweaves the drift of its own nature not because it is nice and reliable, but because we are convinced that it has its own brand of integrity.

The fluid technique of *Hail and Farewell* owes much to Moore's presentation of Gogarty's moral realisation in *The Lake*. And *The Untilled Field* was the ground he worked over before he could find depth to overcome the 'difficulty'.

Moore left Ireland on a grey windless morning in February 1911. He was going back to England. He had, briefly, found a sense of participation in shaping Ireland's destiny; he had also found disillusion, stagnancy, attitudinizing. Begun out of a sense of duty, the stories of *The Untilled Field* became a study of the various tyrannies imposed upon life in Ireland by the church, by false belief, by the mediocrity of convention. In *The Lake* the narrative opened up to the fluidity of consciousness and the life of instinct, and showed the way to *Hail and Farewell*. In Ireland Moore discovered himself as he always was: a storyteller.

TURGENEV AND MOORE: *A SPORTSMAN'S SKETCHES* AND *THE UNTILLED FIELD*

Richard Allen Cave

Writing to an admirer who had expressed dissatisfaction with *The Untilled Field*, Moore advised: 'You will like it better when you take it up six months hence. It is a dry book and does not claim the affections at once.'[1] 'Dry' is a challenging epithet: the context invests the word with the sense of restrained emotion and of quiet humour, of a pithiness and density of texture that will yield up their significance only through a sustained familiarity with the stories. Moore implies his reader is right to be troubled and must herself work to find the meaning. This 'dryness' was a new departure for Moore after the self-conscious flamboyance with which *Evelyn Innes* and *Sister Teresa* had been composed — mere externalities was Moore's preferred way of dismissing them: with all their purple prose they were aridly cerebral; the 'dryness' of *The Untilled Field* was a method designed to achieve a greater inwardness and warmth.

Moore informs us in his Preface to the stories that he took Turgenev's *A Sportsman's Sketches* as his model on the suggestion of John Eglinton. In *Hail and Farewell* he tells how Clara Christian ('Stella') urges him to take Eglinton's chance intuition seriously and how, when he discussed the project with Father Tom Finlay in whose *New Ireland Review* some of the tales first appeared in Gaelic translation, Turgenev very much influenced their talk.[2] Moore was given to sudden enthusiasms but Turgenev he had long admired and, interestingly, an essay on the Russian written back in 1888 helps further to elucidate that epithet 'dry'. His innovation of a new style of short-story writing was, for

Moore, Turgenev's greatest achievement. Trying to define the unique quality of the tales, Moore writes: 'And what is still more marvellous perhaps is that a mere narrative, I will say a bare narrative, should possess the same intellectual charms as the psychological novel', yet the execution is invariably 'light, facile, . . . certain'.[3] For Henry James too that 'bareness' was excitingly deceptive: 'As we read, we are always looking and listening; and we seem, indeed, at moments, for want of a running thread of explanation, to see rather more than we understand.'[4] Explanations the reader must apply himself out of a sensitive engagement with what Moore variously calls the 'indications' and the 'instrumentation' of the storyline. Most writers on Turgenev comment on his extraordinary powers of observation; Moore and James stress rather his meticulously controlled powers of selection, what Conrad later was to call Turgenev's 'unerring instinct for the significant',[5] though Moore would no doubt have added that that significance in no way strains after the reader's attention. Of Turgenev's prose Moore wrote: 'no one phrase is remarkable or striking when read separately, but when taken with the context continues the picture — a picture tense with emotion'.[6] It is because his mastery of his material is so exact that he can 'lead the reader at will'; he does not need to describe feelings or analyse mental attitudes because that mastery is so thorough that he has an absolute confidence in the reader's ability to make scrupulous inferences. Turgenev's tales at once solicit and flatter the reader's imagination. Here is richness in austerity: Moore's 'dryness'.

A good example of Turgenev's technique can be found in 'Yermolai and the Miller's Wife', one of the earliest of the Sketches.[7] The narrator, a hunter, describes in detail a particular kind of shoot, the factual accuracy of it all offset by an account of the heightened sensitivity the Sportsman experiences while in a state of tense expectation; he turns next to his serf companion, Yermolai, a ne'er-do-well, who lives on his wits and his prowess. After an evening expedition, they seek shelter for the night at a nearby mill, are refused entry but later are accommodated in a rough outbuilding in the fields. The miller's wife brings provisions and the narrator sleeps while supper is prepared. He wakes and silently observes the wife's listless posture and large mournful eyes as they are caught in the firelight. She and Yermolai are engaged in a desultory conversation; addressing her with surprising familiarity as 'my darling', he asks for vodka, sings a romantic song absentmindedly while she is away and drinks the proffered spirits at a draught. The woman admits to a continuing illness; Yermolai advises her not to consult a doctor, then urges: 'Come and pay me a visit. . . . I will drive my wife out for the occasion' (I, p. 32). She tells him to wake his master as the potatoes are baked and the narrator feigns waking up, prevents her going by asking about her life and recognises her as the subject of a tragic tale told him months ago by an acquaintance. She had been cruelly turned out of a household where she was lady's maid when her master discovered she was pregnant. Her marriage was arranged. The narrator recalls her master confiding to him that 'it's no good looking for feeling, for heart, in these people' (I, p. 37). The miller calls his wife home; the narrator talks of her with Yermolai who smiles at mention of her husband, reveals that her child died and her lover was sent into the army. Asked about her illness, he changes the subject quickly, promising 'good sport' on the morrow and advising rest. They bury themselves in hay and sleep.

Perceptions, facts and snatches of conversation make up the tale, yet, without any of the 'machinery of pathos' as James calls it,[8] the tragedy of the wife's emotional deprivation is finely caught — the yearning and desperation implicit in her very figure; the unspecified illness, the product of her misery, which in one sense Yermolai could cure, though the blunt insensitivity of his proposal deeply wounds the girl. Throughout he ignores her shyness and treats her brusquely in accord with what he considers her reputation to imply about her. Her master acts from the same premise but takes a shallow moralistic view. When the narrator talks with Yermolai about the girl, he fends off his master's curiosity (though whether in doing so he is consciously aware of any stirring of guilt is open to question) and registers merely indifference. The tale reveals the girl's heartbreak, and the way her private torment is augmented by the advantage others choose to take of her condition. (The title 'Yermolai and the Miller's Wife' encourages us to take the wide perspective.) Given the sensitivity the narrator reveals throughout, one is left to suppose that ultimately his state is one of painful resignation in his inability to do more than sympathise with the girl's plight, since she remains quite beyond the reach of his pity. Here we have, as James says of all the *Sketches*, 'a capital example of moral meaning giving a sense to form and form giving relief to moral meaning'.[9] None of this psychological interpretation is conveyed by direct analysis, rather (to quote James again) 'the living, moving narrative has so effectually put us in the way of feeling with him that we can be depended upon'.[10]

It is here that one wants to take issue with one of Moore's judgements about Turgenev, namely that 'Turgueneff knew the serf as the gentleman knows the serf'.[11] If the implication of that is that Turgenev's stance is patronisingly superior, then Moore is open to criticism. If it implies on Turgenev's part a creative reserve, then the remark is acutely perceptive. Complete empathy with his subject obliterates social distinctions; his interest, as James realises, is *moral* in the widest sense but his scrupulousness causes him to admit that he cannot present the girl's predicament from her subjective point of view; his knowledge of her has its necessary limits and he prefers to work with the intimations, those soul-revealing touches as Moore terms them, that have encouraged him to engage imaginatively with her misery. This is the key to that apparent 'freedom of psychology'[12] that Moore relishes in the *Sketches*, a kind of humility before the subject, which, in refusing to define and label the woman's identity as readily and grossly as the characters in the tale, makes the shaping of the story a moral act. Just such a freedom resulting from a similarly meticulous scruple in the handling obtains in the finest tales in *The Untilled Field*.[13]

Consider 'The Exile' where the method quite transforms what in outline might appear a sentimental anecdote of two brothers' love for the same girl, Catherine. She is infatuated with Peter, who in an undemonstrative way returns her affection though not with the single-minded ardour that James feels for her. Peter, the better educated brother whose happy-go-lucky attempts at farming excite his father's despair,

decides to work for a place at Maynooth, leaving Catherine
for James's exclusive attention; but James's passion cannot
move her. She enters a convent imitating Peter's decision.
Peter returns disgruntled at his failure to apply himself
successfully to his studies. James accepts the situation and
decides to emigrate leaving the family farm to Peter, confident
that with Catherine's capable help he will manage it reasonably
well. Their father fetches an all-too-willing Catherine home
from the convent and James departs. There is a more complex
plot here than in the Turgenev example but Moore handles it
with tactful discretion so that its developments appear to be
wholly the result of what the characters are in themselves.
Many of the stories in the collection like the companion
novel *The Lake* are concerned to explore the nature of instinct
and in 'The Exile' Moore uses the complications of the plot
to instil an awareness of the power of this 'under-life' as he
calls it.[14] The story actually begins with the father Pat's
anxiety to get the best price possible for his cattle at a
market; he knows that James is the born farmer who will
drive a hard bargain but circumstances compel him to send
Peter with disastrous results. The boys are introduced to us
from their father's viewpoint which is coloured by his prime
concern to ensure his farm has a profitable future. Peter's
decision to go to Maynooth will resolve the tangled affections
of the youngsters to his advantage and he strongly encourages
it on the grounds that Peter needs to choose a way of life for
himself. Peter's motive is the more altruistic wish to ease
James's torment:

> 'I met Catherine on the road, and I could do not less
> than walk as far as her door with her.'
> 'You could do no less than that, Pether,' said James.
> 'And what do you mean by that, James?'
> 'Only this, that it is always the crooked way, Pether;
> for if it had been you that had asked her she would have
> had you and jumping.'
> 'She'd have had me!'
> 'And now, don't you think you had better run after
> her, and ask her if she'll have you?'
> 'It's hurtful, James, you should think such a thing of

me. *I* try to get a girl from you!'

'I didn't mean that, Pether; but if she won't have me, you had better try if you can get her.'

And suddenly Peter felt a resolve come into his heart, and his manner grew exultant.

'I've seen Father Tom, and he said I can pass the examination. I'm going to be a priest.'

And when they were lying down side by side Peter said, 'James, it will be all right.' As there was a great heart-sickness on his brother, he put out his hand. 'As sure as I lie here she will be lying next you before this day twelve-months. Yes, James, in this very bed, lying here where I am lying now.'

'I don't believe it, Pether.'

'I do, then.' (p. 9)

James's quiet despair shows how misplaced is Peter's optimism and that his tone earlier in the exchange does not denote peevish envy as Peter suspects. It is a mark of the depth of his affection for Catherine that he knows her more completely than Peter ever will and senses that she will not submit to having her future shaped for her in this way and that consequently his is to be a tragic lot, whatever his brother may argue to the contrary. His recognition of this is accompanied by no self-pity. Had Peter read the signs offered him more sensitively he too would have appreciated the emptiness of his exultation: earlier in this talk with Catherine he has marvelled at her firmness of purpose and her good sense and afterwards he is left wondering 'why he hadn't told her he was going to Maynooth' (p. 8). Catherine knows herself so surely (both words are repeatedly applied to her) that she refuses to acquiesce to the pattern Peter wishes to impose on their lives; her will frustrated, she elects to suppress it completely by submitting to the duties of a convent. Peter's failure at Maynooth makes a different outcome possible.

It is Pat who realises the necessity of James's emigrating but tactfully he shapes their talk so that the decision appears to be his son's and Pat leaves it to James to tell Peter — this act of altruism has to have a whole-hearted commitment. What impresses in the tale is the characters' acceptance of the situation as it finally evolves. Peter's misplaced act of chivalry, which Pat connives at, was an attempt to shape their four lives against what, inwardly, perhaps unconsciously, they intuited to be the necessary pattern of development, but the fact of that intuition, however misguidedly at first they interpreted it, makes them calm before the eventuality of what is the only proper outcome. Their humility in the face of events invests the characters with a remarkable dignity because of their tender scruple for each other, while instinct is wholly freed to pejorative, egotistical connotations.

As Henry James wrote of Turgenev's love stories: he success-fully avoids sentimentality because he attends to the 'moral interest' within the sentimental one.[15] But like Turgenev, Moore offers the reader only factual statements of actions and events and snatches of conversation; it is for the reader to judge for himself even the tone of the dialogue in relation to its consequences and to infer that moral meaning. Just how fresh an innovation in Irish fiction Moore's 'dry' style was, especially in handling the peasant subject, can be gauged from a comparison of Moore's story with 'The Hungry Death' by his near-contemporary, Rosa Mulholland, which Yeats included in his *Representative Irish Tales* in 1891. This too examines the force of unconscious urges to shape an individual's destiny. Brigid is courted by Coll; she feels an intense passion for him but perversely cannot bring herself to encourage his advances; she too much enjoys being the object of his infatuated pursuit and seems to fear the cooling of his ardour should she succumb, even after their betrothal. The psychology of this and the tensions it creates between the lovers are well conceived and presented through convincing observations and dialogue — so well, in fact, that one begins to resent Miss Mulholland's increasing reliance in this part of her story on authorial commentary to interpret how Brigid and Coll respond to each other, with her growing capricious-ness and his confusion turning inexorably to cold distaste; it is information given rather than dramatically rendered. Moreover the commentary is slyly turned to intimate that the tragic consequences of Brigid's behaviour are to be terrible:

On her side, Brigid saw that she had startled him out of

his ordinary easy humour, and, congratulating herself
on the spirit she had shown, resolved to continue her
present style of proceeding. Not one smile would she
give him, till she had, as she told herself, nearly tormented
him to death. How close she was to keep to the letter of
her resolution could not at this time be foreseen.[16]

The irony here is coyly intrusive and so melodramatic, and
the frequency of such touches robs the outcome which is
indeed tragic of its proper degree of pathos. Altogether the
author is over-painstaking in depicting the stages whereby
one event produces particular consequences and over-zealous
too in helping the reader to perceive the moral of it all: Coll
abandons Brigid for Moya and Brigid becomes vindictively
petty till during a famine that overtakes their community she
is compelled by a nightmare that depicts her expulsion from
heaven to carry her last bowl of meal to the dying Moya;
later Brigid crawls over the earthen floor of the Church to die
beneath the Rood: 'A little more effort, and she would be at
His feet.'[17] The power here has all the time to struggle against
the machinery of pathos to engage the reader's imagination.
Moreover the didactic urgency that accompanies the stress on
pathos prevents the tale becoming for the reader a process of
moral discovery, as happens with the stories by Turgenev and
Moore. 'Obey Nature's laws, be simple and obey; it is the best
that you can do' was Turgenev's philosophy in Moore's view[18]
and the same idea might be said to inform 'The Exile'. With
Turgenev and Moore the moral intention does not circum-
scribe the action nor limit the reader's apprehension of the
characters as with Miss Mulholland's tale. They alert the
reader's imagination to the possibility of that moral intention
but the themes the reader finds in their tales are his own
private responsibility: richness and austerity are wholly
interdependent.

The temptation to direct the reader's intelligence must be
considerable and neither Moore nor Turgenev invariably
resist it. The tales that do admit such intrusions, however,
only increase one's insight into the degree of discipline being
exercised elsewhere. Consider Turgenev's 'The Tryst', a simple
tale of the narrator secretly observing the parting between a

servant-girl and a valet who is leaving for town with their master; he has indulged her passion for him as a passing whim and now has thoughts only for the more sophisticated pleasures of the city. The tale explores her innocence and vulnerability, her lack of the knowledge of how to cope with his new indifference towards her without losing her own dignity. The valet leaves, she weeps profusely, the narrator goes to offer his sympathy but she runs away in fear, scattering the flowers she had gathered for her lover. It is a finely observed moment — the narrator's irresistible impulse to bring comfort where there is such an abject abandonment to grief and his helplessness when the girl sees his intrusion as a further humiliation. The narrator retrieves her flowers and journeys on; a sensuous account of details in the landscape that denote the approach of autumn sensitively implies the bleakness that the girl will experience now in her loss; the empathy the narrator feels for the girl colours his every perception. The story ends:

> I turned homewards; but it was long before the figure of poor Akulina faded out of my mind, and her cornflowers, long since withered, are still in my keeping. (II, p. 105)

How this jars after the delicacy of what has gone before! The first half of the sentence is redundant since it merely states what the narrator's perceptions have already and more imaginatively rendered, while the reference to the cornflowers reduces the complex play of emotions in the story to too sentimental an emblem. The girl excites pity yet the desolation of the moment in which she realises the loss of her innocence is such as to place her quite beyond the reach of anyone's compassion; that is the true source of the pathos in her story and the meticulous control of emotion in the narrative carefully prepares the reader for that final insight. The reference to the faded flowers is an emotionalism that the rest of the tale shows to be indiscreet. It is as if Turgenev has missed the meaning of the epiphany he has so delicately evoked.

Something akin to this disturbs the serenity Moore seeks to establish at the close of 'Almsgiving', one of the first stories he composed for *The Untilled Field*. It examines the nature

of charity and our motives for it; beneath the events of the
narrative which tell of his dealings with a blind beggar, the
narrator undergoes a process of self-discovery. Compelled by
the guilt he feels at perversely withholding his customary
charity from the blind man and failing in his attempts at
justifying his meanness on carefully reasoned moral and
social grounds in quelling an impulse to make restitution to
the beggar, he returns, gives money and engages the old man
in conversation about his life. As he talks (not as the narrator
expects, of the hardships and indigence of his life, but of the
consolations he has found), the patronising superiority that
the narrator realises to his shame had motivated his enquiry
gives place to a subdued kind of joy at man's power of
endurance. The blind man's simple tales excite the narrator's
imagination and through that empathy his own perceptions
are, as it were, cleansed, made pristine and attentive. As in
the Turgenev example, Moore captures this change in the
narrator's sensibility through a passage of natural description
but rather than sustaining this indirect mode of expression,
he begins to try to articulate and define the emotion of the
moment:

> A soft south wind was blowing, and an instinct as soft
> and as gentle filled my heart, and I went towards some
> trees. The new leaves were beginning in the high branches.
> I was sitting where sparrows were building their nests,
> and very soon I seemed to see farther into life than I
> had ever seen before. 'We're here,' I said, 'for the purpose
> of learning what life is, and the blind beggar has taught
> me a great deal, something that I could not have learnt
> out of a book, a deeper truth than any book contains. . .'
> And then I ceased to think, for thinking is a folly when
> a soft south wind is blowing and an instinct as soft and
> as gentle fills the heart. (pp. 199-200)

Through not trusting the reader's sensitivity to the implications of the changes in style within the tale, Moore risks
jeopardising the state of wonder he has evoked by reducing
its meaning to a pedestrian, not to say bathetic, statement,
after which his attempt to recover the mood of serenity

appears as so much self-conscious artistry. The failure in method risks making the narrator's impulse of generosity appear an affectation.

Interestingly one of Turgenev's *Sketches*, 'The Living Relic', pursues this same inner theme of wonder but successfully avoids all unwarranted emotionalism. The narrator takes refuge from the rain in a wattled shack and discovers a paralysed, wizened, mummy-like woman who proves to be one of his mother's former maids, once the most buoyant of personalities and a great singer and dancer. A serious fall has reduced her to her present state. Life in her is confined to the activity of her senses and their sensitivity is remarkable. It emerges that this is the result of an equally remarkable mental discipline on her part — the vestiges of that buoyant temperament — to stop herself from thinking or remembering. That way 'the time goes faster' (II, p. 237). Uncomplaining, she celebrates what few faculties she possesses, rejoicing that she can still sing surely, even if her tone is poor. Her story is told by herself in an utterly calm, matter-of-fact manner. The reader is given no directions how to respond but we note that as he talks with her the narrator changes from an initial embarrassment at the encounter (he asks some thoughtlessly cruel questions about her former lover) to complete self-possession which enables him gently to wipe away her tears with his handkerchief — an intimacy that encourages her to confide in him her strange visions of death and salvation. Dread and pity would be quite misplaced in the presence of such calm, such wholehearted and active piety, which impresses the reader through the way it steadily instils peace in the narrator; he ceases to question her condition and accepts. The wonder of it all is not dissipated by any rhetorical devices. The village overseer, in his final comments about her (the one opinion of her life's story offered within the tale) frankly admits the limits of his comprehension, thereby freeing the reader into a wider imaginative apprehension of Lukerya's self-sufficiency: 'Stricken of God . . . for her sins, one must suppose; but we do not go into that. And as for judging her, no — no, we do not judge her. Let her be!' (II, p. 249).

The creative discipline of 'The Living Relic', Turgenev's

art of 'liberating the people he describes' (to use V.S. Pritchett's terms[19]), can be more readily appreciated from a comparison with the incidents that make up the sketch entitled 'Death'. In the first the narrator while hunting is called on to help save a serf who has been crushed beneath a falling tree; the man's back is broken and shortly after he dies. The manner of his death starts the narrator musing:

> How wonderfully indeed the Russian peasant dies! The temper in which he meets his end cannot be called indifference or stolidity; he dies as though he were performing a solemn rite, coolly and simply. (II, p. 27)

One is up against the deficiencies of translation here, of course;[20] but the use of a simile, the effort to find the exact word and above all the rhetorical exclamation convey a degree of self-consciousness which is not true to the experience that was previously described; it rings false to the very 'moral interest' Turgenev would have us appreciate in the event. Indeed with that first death and with the others that come crowding into the narrator's mind, it is the abnegation of self by the dying personality that excites in those privileged to witness the death that calm, free of self-regarding emotions like dread or embarrassment, that Turgenev evokes so exactly in 'A Living Relic'. Repeating the exclamation about the extraordinary way Russians die after each of the incidents in 'Death' invests the phrase in time with some specific connotations but it remains a disturbingly loose, even trivial judgement drawing attention away from the experience under discussion to the inadequacy of language to define emotional atmosphere by direct statement. Far greater precision lies in Turgenev's art of tentative indications.

That Moore admired Turgenev's portrayals of simplehearted piety is evident from his singling out 'Kassyan of Fair Springs' for detailed comment in his essay of 1888. Here, though the narrator first dismisses Kassyan as 'cracked', longer acquaintance brings him to respect the strange dwarf as an adept in folk medicine and lore and as a mystic. *The Untilled Field* contains several studies of minds that one might initially judge as 'cracked' but which Moore's artistry urges us to view with greater understanding. 'A Letter to Rome' is a fine example of Moore's sureness of ear for tone — a tone here that will best convey the absurdity and the strength of Father McTurnan. His scheme to marry the Catholic clergy to repopulate an Ireland laid desolate by famine and emigration would verge on farce (especially given his own private terror at the thought of ending years of cherished celibacy) were it not for the very real misery amongst his parishioners that compels him to search in desperation for a cure. Ridiculous as his suggestion to the Pope may be, it is the product of a compassion for the poor that he has long since recognised as useless; and it is no more bizarre than current Government schemes to involve his parishioners in building work on the condition that no one individual or class profit by it. Always he works to honour the dignity of the indigent, not allowing himself to let their condition as a social problem dehumanize them in his thinking. To the Inspector's suggestion that the people use the subsidy to build an arch in the middle of the bog, his reply is pointed: 'No, no. A road to the sea will be quite useless; but its futility will not be apparent — at least not so apparent — and the people's hearts won't be broken' (p. 140). That correction reminding himself that his people are intelligent is typical of the man and typical of the way Moore delicately sustains a balance between laughter and pathos; stressing the selfless scruple and the unstinting care of the priest saves the laughter from taking on that tone of derision that implies a superiority to the subject. It is the relentlessness with which the instinct for charity searches for a mode of expression in McTurnan's life that commands respect.

Another story of this type, 'The Window', seems actually to draw on Turgenev's 'The Living Relic' for at least some of its inspirations in depicting a simple but intense piety. Lukerya confiding her visions to the narrator hardly dares to call them that since the priest has told her that 'visions come only to the clerical gentry' (II, p. 246). Moore builds on the satirical implications of this to explore in his tale the divergence between the spirit and the letter of faith. It is frequently a technique of Turgenev's to avoid intruding precise judgements into a story to shape it around two related but contrasting character-studies, each highlighting the limitations of the other and the related strengths.[21] In 'The Living Relic' the overseer's view of Lukerya is a plausible one but is felt by the reader to be misguided, indeed its very inadequacy makes the exercise of his own discrimination imperative. Moore fuses these two techniques in 'The Window' to give us a tale of a priest and a saint. Biddy McHale, a cripple like Lukerya, elects as her life's work to donate a stained glass window to her church and all her energy and faculties are directed to that end. Her singlemindedness might be deemed obsessional were it not for its power to protect her innocence from the wiles of the parish priest, Father Maguire, who is bent on exploiting her modest savings to further his own schemes for rebuilding his church. In exasperation he views her complete simplicity as cunning but the judgement recoils on him. In another of the stories, 'Patchwork', a shrewder priest observes of the peasantry that courtship represents 'all the aspiration that may come into their lives. After they get married, the work of the world grinds all the poetry out of them' (p. 78). Biddy is deprived as a cripple of such an outlet for the 'poetry' in her but working for her objective frees her of any sense of drudgery and when her window is finally installed her joy finds imaginative release in visions. Her serenity is now as absolute and self-consuming as her ambition was formerly. The priest tolerates her when he realises he can use her new reputation as a local saint to foster subscriptions to his building-fund; but to the last she remains a thorn in his flesh, perplexing him as to 'what her happiness might be' (p. 130). It is the tragi-comic undertow to the story that Biddy's essential goodness, so free from any taint of practised piety, excites in the priest cupidity, anger and envy. He sees but he cannot believe; she believes and what she sees is transfigured. Turgenev communicates Lukerya's joy through her dialogue with the narrator; Moore's narrator is an omniscient recorder, so he conveys the quality of Biddy's perceptions through the rhythm and simple phrasing of his prose, the matter-of-fact portrayal of the wondrous capturing perfectly Biddy's loss of self-consciousness as she enters a transcendent reality.

The anti-clerical satire is stronger in Moore's story of

course than in Turgenev's, though it is held in control by the larger imaginative focus which places elsewhere the moral interest of the tale; it is in no way stressed and what view the reader takes of Father Maguire emerges wholly out of the interplay of his personality with Biddy's. Similarly in 'Patchwork', though a priest is the butt of the comic situation, the criticism of him is voiced by an older priest who is quietly bemused at his inexperience. If the priests are shown to be fallible, they are nonetheless tolerated as men, as are the landlords who are the subject of much criticism, direct and implied, in *A Sportsman's Sketches*. Turgenev does not allow judgement to restrict his curiosity about character. If 'The Wild Goose' and 'Fugitives' appear oddly out of place in *The Untilled Field*, it is because the anti-clerical feeling has become dominant at the expense of Moore's 'dry' style.[22] Opinions, rather than a hesitating attempt to give expression to complex feelings, form the substance of the conversations (and opinions that, from the development of the stories, Moore clearly wishes the reader to endorse) with the result that though these tales are longer than the others in the volume they are more restricted in scope, for the reader is no longer required to engage with the artistry of their method and work imaginatively to find the meaning. From Moore's letters to his publisher, Fisher Unwin, and from the discussion about 'The Wild Goose' with Edward Martyn that is included in *Hail and Farewell* one can gauge how Moore deliberately set out to be contentious and this produces writing that is both ugly and slack.[23] Techniques of foreshadowing events in the plot, such as 'he felt sure that his opinions, as soon as they were fully realised by her, would cleave their love as a hatchet cleaves the wood' (p. 280), bring a mechanical quality to the narrative quite absent from the earlier tales while the crude metaphor alienates even further. Ned Carmady sees himself as Ireland's political Messiah but he decides to leave the country when his views arouse clerical opposition to the point where he finds the intellectual life of Dublin too restrictive because too subservient to Catholic orthodoxy. But Carmady's views as iterated at length in the tale do not convince the reader as being in any way specially enlightened, rather they are simply combative, and stridently so at that.

Moore is not speaking for the character but through him.

The basic situation of an earlier story, 'Home Sickness', is exactly the same as 'The Wild Goose': a returning emigrant; his emotional involvement with an Irish woman; their separation when he finds the quality of Irish life claustrophobic; his choice of America as his true home. Though a parish priest vigorously condemns the drinking and dancing that Bryden's money can buy for the villagers to celebrate his courting of Margaret Dirken, more than that shapes his decision to go back to the Bowery: it is the joyless drudgery of the peasant farmers working their smallholdings for a pittance; the hard, unyielding landscape; and the meanspiritedness and self-pity these seem together to induce in the villagers that afflict him. He pities them but comes to dread sharing their condition. Throughout the tale Moore reiterates the adjective 'small' and subtly uses it to chart a significant change in Bryden's perceptions: at first it implies a delight in the different and the unusual, the recovery of an Ireland his memory had played tricks with during his stay in New York; later the smallness impinges and constricts, taking on metaphorical overtones. When Bryden sees about him 'worn fields divided by walls of loose stones' (p. 45), the quality of his perception intimates his own slow breaking down to the pattern of spiritual greyness common to the villagers if he should stay. His decision to leave is inevitable but the inevitability is not brought about by a mechanical manipulating of the plot, rather it is conveyed as an instinctive response that steadily colours Bryden's every perception till it becomes an irresistible compulsion. The tale evokes a movement of the total consciousness; Bryden's decision, unlike Carmady's, is not merely an intellectual matter; and 'Home Sickness' is suffused with social awareness rather than social criticism. That, despite its brevity, is its strength. The lack of social awareness to substantiate the ideas at play in 'The Wild Goose' and 'Fugitives' is what makes them seem little more than shallow opinionating. When Moore loses his hold on Turgenev's method, his own artistry suffers.

One major difference between the *Sketches* and *The Untilled Field* (as much of the foregoing should substantiate) lies in how the actual narration is handled. Turgenev characterises himself as the narrator; he writes in the first-person as a landlord whose passion for shooting game has given him a profound sensitivity to natural phenomena which makes his further enlightenment about the unique individuality of the serfs wholly credible. Only 'Almsgiving' imitates Turgenev's technique and that not with complete success; Moore's general habit is to take an omniscient stance. Other tales by Turgenev experiment with the device of the characterised narrator to a more sophisticated level. A particular favourite of Moore's was 'Lear of the Steppes' where the story is told by an elderly man out of his recollections of events that occurred during his adolescence when he was impressed by the strangeness of behaviour in a neighbouring household without being able to understand the emotional undercurrent that gave it its meaning and logic. When Kharloff, the Lear-figure, dies tearing apart the roof of the homestead from which he has been expelled by his daughters, the youth is shocked into a sudden clarity of apprehension of how everyone else is responding to the death; he begins to make connections and understand that details of posture, vocal tones and spatial relations between individuals carry very precise psychological connotations. The old man's death marks the boy's growth to adulthood. Moore attempted nothing as complex as this within *The Untilled Field*, though the companion-novel, *The Lake*, employs a similar technique of defining psychological growth through recording from a subjective stance the changing relations between perception and understanding. When Moore treats the theme of a young girl's access to adulthood through confronting and conquering her fear of death in 'The Wedding Gown', it is handled quite objectively except for the moment of confrontation when in the rhythms of the prose Moore captures first the breathless haste of Molly's race through the dark to her home and then the studied calm that comes over her when she faces her great-aunt's body and recognises there not only the physical resemblance with herself but the fact of their common mortality. Through his control of the rhythmic modulations Moore achieves a complete empathy with his character.[24]

Only one of the stories, 'A Playhouse in the Waste',

attempts a sophisticated narrative framework and that to explore how thinly in a remote rural community a veneer of Christianity covers a more primitive superstition and retributive moral code.[25] The subject is once again Father McTurnan and the tale opens with the derision of a circle of Dublin intellectuals who have heard rumours of his letter to Rome. News of a new exploit — building a theatre on the bog — provokes more scoffing till one of the group shocks the rest to silence with an account of visiting the priest and finding him strangely withdrawn and nervous, and painfully embarrassed at being asked to guide the narrator to the playhouse. Effortlessly Moore shifts the tone from the risible to the eerie as the narrator tells how unsettled he was on his night-time journey to McTurnan's parish by the superstitious hysteria of the jarvey and his companion and later by the tension lying behind the priest's unwillingness to talk about his projects or his flock. More disturbing still given his previous alarm is the jarvey's unemotional and unquestioning explanation for it all with his tale of the murder that was the utterly illogical consequence of building the playhouse, which has left McTurnan broken and a prey to guilt. The intricate structure of stories within the story incline the reader to accept the peasants' belief in the supernatural and superstitious with complete seriousness but also to deflect his attention away from the terrible events of the tale to their tragic psychological implications for McTurnan given what we know from the previous story of his scrupulous conscience. It is absurd that he should feel incriminated by having provided, unwittingly, the occasion for the tragedy, but it is the mark of his tender sense of responsibility towards his parish that he does. What is best in him has brought about his complete humiliation: like the playhouse, which is its token, the instinct for charity, the most fundamental aspect of his identity, is laid waste. Effecting the transition to tragic proportions of a character deemed at first an endearing eccentric is made possible by the carefully judged complexity of the narrative framework and by the assured modulations in tone. One is reminded here of Flaubert's comment on Turgenev: 'You never strain for dramatic situations, yet you obtain tragic effects by the sheer finish of the composition.'[26] That is precisely what Moore meant by his 'dry' style — the confidence in one's mastery of the subject that gains one immediate and unforced access to the reader's imagination and sensibility; a style too where the sheer finish of the artistry is the mark of the author's whole-hearted compassion. 'Dryness', as Moore assured his correspondent, does not mean that the fiction lays no claim to the reader's affections. Similarly Flaubert saw that praise of Turgenev's method did not do full justice to his genius: 'But one thing about you has never had sufficient praise, your heart; your unfailing feeling, I mean, your indescribable deep and hidden sensibility.'[27]

'A NAKED GAEL SCREAMING "BRIAN BORU"'[1]

Tomás Ó Murchadha

I

'Ireland and I have ever been strangers, without an idea in common. It never does an Irishman any good to return to Ireland' (p. 77). So George Moore told Yeats and Edward Martyn when they came to see him in Victoria Street in London. On the surface at least it did not seem a propitious occasion: Yeats, a dreamy aristocratic poet, and Martyn, a stolid Catholic, approaching an ex-Catholic Anglo/Francophile with the idea of founding a Literary Theatre in Dublin. 'Like giving a mule a holiday' (p. 77) was Moore's first reaction. Yeats was reprimanded for tilting his chair dangerously, Martyn became defiant, and the visitors declined an invitation to dinner.

But that strange occasion was the beginning of the Abbey Theatre, and the beginning of George Moore's ten-year pilgrimage to Ireland, out of which came *The Untilled Field* and *The Lake*.

Moore was the most reluctant of Gaels. Ireland represented ignorance, philistinism, and the Catholicism he hated. But Yeats and Martyn had fanned a flame: something was happening in Ireland; excitement and revolution were in the air; there was even talk of a Renaissance, 'a new language to en-womb new thoughts' (p. 55). *Hail and Farewell* chronicles the rise of that irresistible urge:

I became possessed by a sentimental craving for the country itself. After all, it was my country. . . (p. 208)

But as he goes deeper into the bog:

I began to tremble lest the terrible Cathleen ni Houlihan might overtake me. She had come out of that arid plain, out of the mist, to tempt me, to soothe me into forget-fulness that it is the plain duty of every Irishman to disassociate himself from all memories of Ireland — Ireland being a fatal disease, fatal to Englishmen and doubly fatal to Irishmen. (p. 213)

But the uneasy enthusiasm for Ireland grew, and his disgust with the Boer war and England's role in it began to corrode his love of the English way of life. He realised that he wanted victory for the Boers and finally that:

the Englishman that was in me (he that wrote Esther Waters) had been overtaken and captured by the Irish-man. (pp. 215-6)

Having fought Cathleen ni Houlihan bitterly through several frustrating and some absurd visits to Ireland, the call became overwhelming, reaching an almost supernatural intensity:

Of this I am sure — that the words Go to Ireland did not come from within, but from without . . . the Messiah Ireland was waiting for was in me and not in another. (p. 257)

And so the man who had discovered himself a Hibernophile with some reluctance, set out to find Ireland, wondering if it would be 'small as a pig's back' or a land of 'extraordinary enchantment'. (p. 107)

The Renaissance had begun. Yeats, Synge, Lady Gregory, A.E., Hyde, were staking out their literary ground; Stephens, Joyce, O'Casey and others were poised to do so. Patrick Pearse was twenty years old. But Moore's contribution was to be entirely different from that of any of the others, in style, in language, and in thought content. His espousal of Cathleen never reached the colourful and romantic heights of some of her other suitors. *The Untilled Field* is far from being a lyrical panegyric. Indeed, apart from Joyce there is little criticism of the old sow as severe.

The fact is that Moore returned to Ireland not just to join the literary bandwagon, not just to find a new language. He was looking for something in life that was eluding him — some kind of salvation or redemption, some kind of at-one-ment with day to day living. While he was crying out his paganism, his anti-clericalism, and eventually his Protestantism, he was longing for some kind of central spiritual transformation in his life. He fell under the spell of A.E., and hoped that the revolutionary spirit of the times and the mysticism of A.E. would lead him to his goal. (There is a charming tale of Moore and A.E. setting out on their bicycles to visit the Newgrange burial-mound in the belief that they would attain some kind of spiritual vision there.)

It was this unconscious need which troubled Moore, and which made him such a volatile man; his anger at the corrupt clergy, the antics with the Gaelic League, his disillusion with England, these were only symptoms. This trouble is reflected in *The Untilled Field* in a certain reluctance to face his own responses. In *The Lake* he comes closer to naming the problem: 'the mysterious warble, soft as lake water, that abides in the heart.'[2]

Even Moore's friends seem to have been aware of an unease in him, expressed particularly in his ambivalence about Ireland: 'In Ireland we don't mean all we say, that is your difficulty', Yeats is recorded as saying to him in *Hail and Farewell*, which words, Moore says 'appeased' him (p. 109). Later Moore has Yeats say: 'I know Ireland better than you, and am more patient' (p. 126). Of course these words were written by Moore after the event, when his pilgrimage was over, and when he knew more about his malaise:

It is hard to analyse a spiritual transformation: one knows little about oneself; life is mysterious. (p. 216)

He went, then, not just to write a book 'in the hope of furnishing the young Irish of the future with models',[3] but out of a deeper instinct for what he conceives as a 'spiritual transformation'. It was a Messianic impulse, and Ireland was to be the Israel of Moore's transforming zeal.

His pilgrimage may have failed in that he did not redeem

Ireland from its mortal sins of ignorance and philistinism, but without this experience, without having written *The Untilled Field* and *The Lake*, he could never have gone on to write *The Brook Kerith*, in which he finally achieved mastery of cool detached narrative.

II

It was the peasants and the priests of rural Ireland that most captured Moore's fascination. The peasants were the repositories of the Irish language, and the possible source of a primeval peace or excitement which might inspire a new literature. *The Untilled Field* seethes with the life of these people, with their everyday affairs, their traumas and their burdens. Often they are observed by an outsider, a returned exile, a visitor to the parish, or an artist.

'He strolled on interested in Ireland's slattern life, touched by the kindness and simplicity of the people' (p. 217). This is Ned Carmady in 'The Wild Goose', observing and seeking out the genius of the Irish people for his American newspaper. But already there are disturbing signs: 'The art of verbal expression has been denied them', he mutters as he strolls through the village. The fair is seething with life and affability, but Carmady does not fit in — he fails in his encounters with the dealers and jobbers, is laughed at, and is unable to stand the smell of the taproom. His thoughts on The Celt are already slightly tarnished.

James Bryden (in 'Home Sickness') returns to his native land in search of health after many years in a New York bar. He finds the people poorer than when he left them, more miserably dispirited than he remembered: 'their talk was as depressing as their appearance, and he could feel no interest whatever in them' (p. 37). They are ragged, unhealthy, interested only in their own trivial affairs, their one regret being that they did not go to America when they were young. Bryden soon wearies of them, and begins to wish himself back in the Bowery. Lying on his bed in Mike Scully's loft on his first night home 'he seemed to realise suddenly how lonely the country was, and he foresaw mile after mile of scanty fields stretching all round the lake with one little town in the far corner. . . His terror increased, and he drew the blanket over his head' (p. 38). In the confrontation with the priest at the house-dance, the peasants, far from standing out against the tyrant, add insult to injury by handing Bryden's umbrella to their tormentor. A letter brings the smell of the Bowery slum across the Atlantic to Bryden, and he is compelled to take precipitate flight.

In the 'Some Parishioners' sequence ('Some Parishioners', 'Patchwork', 'The Wedding Feast', 'The Window') Moore develops his anti-clericalism and his view of the weakness of the peasants: 'The sexes mix freely everywhere in Western Europe; only in Ireland and Turkey is there any attempt made to separate them' (p. 51), says the sympathetic Fr. Stafford. The handling of the poultry-keeping lecture by Fr. Maguire borders on being incredible. But the peasants are totally stricken before him, totally without strength or backbone, craven and deferential before his insatiable and outrageous demands: 'Kate Kavanagh won't go home until she promises to marry Peter. I have had enough of her goings on in my parish' (p. 51), and Kate trembles before him.

Kate is the only one of 'the low Irish' who has any spirit or strength but Moore does not bring us close enough to her to feel any great sympathy. She is a bit brassy, in fact, but at least she has the gumption to leave — the only possible salvation for these wretched creatures. By the time Pat Connex stops her on the road, worried that she might be asking him to sin with her, we are thoroughly weary of them. As Connex says, 'We're a dead and alive lot,' and we must surely agree with him.

There is an intention in this book which is not just literary, but didactic. Moore wanted to show the Irish people to themselves, hoping to provoke a reaction. More than to 'serve as a model' for future writers, he wanted to kindle a flame.

But Moore's sympathy for the peasants often comes closer to pity or even contempt than to real warmth or empathy. One wonders if Moore himself was aware of this rupture. It arose from a hatred of the 'poor mouth' mentality that so

often goes with poverty, and for the vulgarity and superstition that Moore considered went with Irish Catholicism,
coupled with a genuine love for the peasants themselves, and
his own urgent need to understand them.

It could be said that Myles na gCopaleen (Flann O'Brien)
wrote his great Gaelic satire *An Béal Bocht* out of the same
instincts that produced *The Untilled Field*, i.e. a mixture of
love for the people, a rage at their weaknesses, and a deep
respect. The difference was that Myles knew his subject more
intimately than Moore did; their language, their Gaelic literature, their habits and vagaries were in his very bones — a
part of his own nature in fact. Myles found the safest and
probably the only way of facing the dilemma — laughter.
An Béal Bocht is a savage indictment of Gaelic and peasant
ways, but because of its virtue of laughter (black and painful though it may be at times) it is a more lovable book than
The Untilled Field. One is tempted to speculate to what
extent Myles na gCopaleen was one of Moore's projected heirs.

Turgenev also had preoccupations with peasant *mores*, and
is mentioned by Moore himself as a progenitor of *The Untilled
Field*, and of course he is, both in style and subject matter.
But Turgenev also knew his peasants better than Moore did.
He spent more time with them and mixed with them. He did
not have the unease bordering on repugnance which Moore
had, and which Fr. Gogarty in *The Lake* has to deal with in
himself: a 'sinful dislike of poverty he overcame in early
manhood' (p. 53).

This 'sinful dislike' is close to the centre of Moore's unease. Not until he faces it does his work acquire the centrality
of ease and mastery that he wished for.

We glimpse Moore's troubled vision in 'The Window' when
Fr. Maguire and a young man, a stranger in the village, interested in ecclesiastical art, stand watching poor old Biddy
M'Hale dreaming her strange and beautiful dreams before
her window:

> 'Look at her', said the young man. 'Can you doubt that
> she sees heaven quite plainly, and that the saints visited
> her just as she told us? . . . Be patient with her: let her
> enjoy her happiness.'

> And the two men stood looking at her, trying vainly to
> imagine what her happiness might be. (pp. 129-30)

One cannot resist seeing Moore himself as just such a bemused
observer, 'trying vainly to imagine' what the mind of the
peasant is, trying to find the 'unchanging silent life' in the
rocky and untilled field of the peasant soul. Here is the
tension: the untilled and unwashed spirit of Ireland is what
Moore finds at once alluring and repulsive. It is at once
ignoble and mysterious, glorious and elusive.

Moore's sympathy and love of the peasants cannot be ques-
tioned after reading 'The Exile', a story full of warmth,
pathos and humanity. But Moore was attempting to transcend
earthly human sympathy in its day-to-day context. He was
looking for something elemental and sublime. The fact is that
he had less in common with the peasants (and they with
him) than with the landlord class (note the splendid generosity
of the landlord in 'Home Sickness', in turning over no less
than twenty acres of pasture to Bryden, in one almost off-
hand gesture making Bryden a rich man!). And Moore had
still more in common with that very class he despised — the
priests.

It is only when he faces this dilemma, cutting through
the wretchedness that so inflamed him, and concentrating
on the kind of people he understands, that he can bask in
the true light of his vision. It is in *The Lake*, by the expedient
of making a priest his hero, that Moore finds his freedom. And
it is not on any scrubby field, tilled or otherwise, that Fr.
Gogarty finds redemption, but on lake water.

III

Moore's heroes, whatever their faults, all have to deal with
their uneasy conscience. Moore brings them face to face with
the patchwork nature of human resolution, with the cyclic
and wandering human mind and wishes. The cruel Fr. Maguire
in the 'Some Parishioners' sequence, becomes almost obsessed

with his guilt, to the extent that he commits the same sin twice: having forced one bad match he goes on, obsessively 'hypnotising' Fr. Stafford into assisting him in his efforts. The second forced marriage is an even greater disaster than the first.

Bryden, hero of 'Home Sickness', also falls victim twice, returning to home sickness for Ireland in the end of his life, and the very landscape he remembers reflects his spiritual state:

> and the things he saw most clearly were the green hillside, and the bog lake and the rushes about it, and the greater lake in the distance, and behind it the blue line of wandering hills. (p. 49)

Bryden has to deal with the consequences of an irrevocable decision, the wrong he did to Margaret Dirken (and to Ireland) when he fled all those years before.

The gentle Fr. MacTurnan, while fulfilling God's plan by gently and stoically trying to do good for his parish ('A Playhouse in the Waste'), is tormented by storms that might have been God's design, and by the ghost of an unbaptised baby. His bizarre plan to save Ireland from Protestantism ('A Letter to Rome') becomes an obsession that could ruin him.

Ellen in 'The Wild Goose' states ' "If I weren't (a Catholic) I'm afraid I'd be very wicked" ' and Ned has to fly from the 'base moral coinage'.

Fr. Maguire, Fr. MacTurnan and Fr. Gogarty all declare that celibacy is no burden to them. Moore knows otherwise, and puts them to the test.

The clerk in 'The Clerk's Quest' becomes obsessed with his unknown love to the point of fetish. The hero of 'Almsgiving' becomes obsessed with his intolerance 'for all life but my own', and reflects that 'our motives are vague, complex, and many'.

All these people are in one way or another alienated from themselves or from the world they inhabit. They are exiles, in a sense, among their own people. Exile, in one form or another, is the abiding theme of *The Untilled Field*. The book is full of these exiles, from the first story to the last. They are uneasy, anxious people, often obsessed, often unhappy. The story 'So on He Fares' is not only a splendid description of exile and the concomitant urgent need to return to roots, it is a powerful comment on the inevitable cyclicity of human nature, and on the impossibility of fulfilling this need to return. Having found the image of himself as a child he goes *for the second time* into exile. And again the landscape reflects the inevitable round:

> The evening sky opened calm and benedictive, and the green country flowed, the boat passed by ruins, castles and churches, and every day was alike until they reached the Shannon. (p. 216)

Here, as in *The Lake*, it is water that imparts freedom.

Moore's characters are searching for themselves, as Moore was searching for himself, as Shakespeare was through his characters, as any writer is. Moore felt himself to be an intellectual and spiritual exile among his fellows, and nowhere was this more painfully obvious than in Ireland. He set his characters on the road to self-knowledge and to reconciliation with that self. That was his pilgrimage; that was what made him irrevocably a writer.

But in the midst of Moore's most serious encounters with life he is wont to introduce a note of frivolity, as when he hears, like St. Patrick, the voice calling him to Ireland:

> I walked, greatly shaken in my mind, feeling that it would be impossible for me to keep my appointment with the lady who had asked me to tea that evening. (*Hail and Farewell*, p. 257)

At a dinner in Dublin, in the presence of Hyde, Yeats, John O'Leary and many of the most renowned personages of the time, Moore can muse maliciously: 'Perhaps they haven't even changed their socks' (p. 128). This is no more than the delicious malice Moore would have dabbled with in Paris as a young man, and it is this quality, tempered by irony, which makes *Hail and Farewell* so readable.

In the stories 'In the Clay' and 'The Way Back', later re-constituted as 'Fugitives', the sculptor Rodney — a man of some sophistication — when his statue is broken describes Ireland as 'an unwashed country' and later two priests ruminating over tumblers of whiskey decide that: 'Bad statues were more likely to excite devotional feelings than good ones, bad statues being further removed from perilous nature' (p. 310). Meanwhile the case of Ireland, as put by Harding, is a colourless and unconvincing one, intellectually limp, morally weak. Moore, who valued art as the most direct encountering of life, would rank this consideration of bad art as most damning. But Moore himself seems to have been un-easy with this story, shown by his rather unsuccessful re-writing and reconstituting.

Moore's difficulty in finding a relationship with Ireland really reflects his own search into the more mysterious and inchoate aspects of his own psyche. He is at his best when attempting to probe the metaphysical shadows. He came to Ireland as an explorer, as Darwin went to Patagonia. Explorers of deserts (and what else is the untilled field?) may find within themselves a primeval calm which is also known to the savage inhabitants, and which may lead them to the peace of God. His pilgrimage was not an entirely secular one. In *Hail and Farewell* he not only refers to a 'spiritual transformation' but to 'a new self'. 'Into what life will it lead me?', he ponders in some alarm, 'Into what Christianity?' (p. 216).

'Yeats and Edward are both addicted to magic' Moore reflects, 'it matters little that each cultivates a different magic' (p. 91). In his own way Moore was also interested in raising himself, like a magus (or a priest), out of ordinary everyday life into an intenser one. *The Untilled Field* reaches its highest points when he attempts this transformation, the spare simple language becomes a super-efficient fuel to the soaring imagination.

When Dempsey in 'The Clerk's Quest' lies down for the last time to let his obsession expire he is blessed by an imaginative genuflection of nature itself: 'it seemed to him that one of the stars came down from the sky and laid its bright face upon his shoulder' (p. 193). When the gentleman in 'Almsgiving' yields to his heart and helps the poor beggar he also is blessed by nature:

> And then I ceased to think, for thinking is a folly when
> a soft south wind is blowing and an instinct as soft and
> as gentle fills the heart. (p. 200)

Biddy M'Hale's glorious dream before her window of saints and angels, the 'white thing' which is the ghost of the unbaptised baby, the curse of Julia Cahill, are among the most haunting things in the book.

But the supernatural was not the end, for Moore was neither a mystic nor a metaphysician. In the final analysis it is the human that matters. Perhaps the most positive, most successful moment of the book is when poor Fr. MacTurnan returns late at night to his parishioner James Murdoch with the price of not one, but two pigs, which will enable him to marry. The priest in his enthusiasm and joy, entirely forgetful now of his grievous obsession, drags him from his bed and 'The poor man came stumbling across the bog, and the priest told him the news' (p. 149).

Moore never allows the human to escape him. It is his greatest quality as a writer that he always keeps his characters right before his eyes, in firm view.

Ned Carmady, in 'The Wild Goose', is 'filled with an awe and an ecstacy' while watching the wild geese at Howth, and considering Ireland's great era of Christianity ('"Will it ever come again?" he asked') is brought to earth by a shepherd's folk-tune. It becomes a symbol of Ireland itself — 'no words can describe its melancholy. . . It is the song of the exile, the cry of one driven out into a night of wind and rain, a prophetic echo.' And Ned goes into exile:

> possessed by the great yearning of the wild goose when
> it rises from the warm marshes, scenting the harsh north
> through leagues of air, and goes away on steady wing-
> beats. (p. 280)

Steadily Ned goes, and he is 'overjoyed that he has done it'. Religion is 'a development of the romance which begins on earth' (*Hail and Farewell*, p. 158), and every man is a pagan, albeit overlaid with Christianity. Man has a powerful longing to awaken this primeval paganism, to break free, to share in some way in wild nature's round. Ned Carmady achieves this apotheosis as he watches 'the green waves tossing in the mist' while Howth melts into the 'grey drift'. It is the high point of the book, the target of Moore's endeavour.

In *The Lake* a priest, having struggled with his conscience, his passions, his vocation and his God, throws himself naked into the purifying element of water, and finds the same release.

IV

The Lake was meant to be included as a story in *The Untilled Field* but in the event was not published until two years later, in 1905. This was 'a mistake' (p. ix) according to Moore, though he continued to allow it to stand as a novel in its own right through subsequent editions. It is the proper completion of the earlier book, and both lose considerably in 'range and power' (Moore's words) if not considered together. They arise from the same stimulus and have the same aim. If the high point of *The Untilled Field* is Carmady's release in 'The Wild Goose', Fr. Oliver Gogarty's escape at the end of *The Lake* is a parallel, but a much deeper and fuller one, and more successfully wrought.

We have already seen how *The Untilled Field* was revised several times. Moore himself seems to have been uneasy about the book. He wrote it, he tells us, 'in the beginning out of no desire for self-expression', a strange idea indeed, and one which, as T.R. Henn has pointed out (*The Untilled Field*, p. v), we need not take too seriously. There is a dramatic structure to the book's logic. Beginning close to the peasants in 'The Exile' we see the problem of exile through their eyes, unobserved by any outsider; in the second story we see the problem through the eyes of Bryden, who is more aware, having been through it himself. Next, in the 'Some Parishioners' sequence, we are with the peasants again, but with the important difference of the priest's presence. He is a man of some awareness and vision, albeit twisted. The theme continues through until it finds it fullest statement in 'So on He Fares' and eventually to its resolution in 'The Wild Goose'.

The Lake is in a sense a re-statement of all that is in *The Untilled Field*, but a fuller one in that it is worked out in the spirit of a single human being. The questions of intolerance, intellectual and spiritual freedom, primeval longing, faith, rigorous self-examination are all here, wrapped in one personality. 'Every man has a lake in his heart', Fr. Oliver muses, and it is this lake which Moore is exploring in this novel. This time there is no external dimension of Ireland, no untilled desert. It is a personal matter, and the priest's breakthrough to self-hood involves plunging into that lake of self and crossing it. Moore successfully carries us across the lake, and thus prepares the way for himself to move even beyond it. Moore had to achieve that crossing in himself, he had to explore and conquer that part of himself, before he could write his masterpiece, *The Brook Kerith*.

Before the story of *The Lake* opens Nora Glynn has been dismissed from her teaching post, having become pregnant. Fr. Oliver has preached a sermon against her and she has left the parish for England, where, Fr. Oliver fears, her faith may be in peril. He begins a tortured progression of letters until he realises he is in love with her. He loses his faith and finally escapes by feigning his drowning, swimming across the lake to freedom and exile. Moore brings us step by step through the man's torment until he finally admits that he has ceased to believe and that he must leave. The lake, always reflecting his nervous state, now becomes a kind of celestial lake, mirroring the harmony he has found:

> The moment was one of extraordinary sweetness; never might such a moment happen in his life again. And he watched the earth and sky enfolded in one tender harmony of rose and blue — blue fading to grey, and the lake afloat amid vague shores, receding like a dream through sleep. (p. 139)

He writes his plan to Nora, 'everyone must try to cling to his own soul'.

The swim of freedom contains some of Moore's finest writing, and the book, like *The Untilled Field*, ends on water:

On the deck of the steamer he heard the lake's warble above the violence of the waves. 'There is a lake in every man's heart,' he said, 'and he listens to its monotonous whisper year by year, more and more attentive till at last he ungirds.' (p. 179)

It was over ten years later that Moore published *The Brook Kerith*. In this book he takes us, in a sense, across the lake and beyond. Life goes on after the grand gesture has been made, as if we had followed Fr. Oliver to America and seen his life there.

In *The Brook Kerith* Jesus recovers after the crucifixion and lives on among his friends the Essene monks with whom he had been for many years before he began his miracle-working. We see his life tending his sheep in contentment until he meets Paul of Tarsus when he (Jesus) is aged fifty three. Taking pity on Paul (who believes this old shepherd to be a madman) he tells him:

The world will always be idolatrous. All things are God, Paul. . . in some sort of fashion. . . There is but one thing: to learn to live for ourselves, and to suffer our fellows to do likewise.[4]

Paul leaves for Rome, and we can assume that Jesus will join a group of Indian monks who are preaching in Caesarea. This is no grand gesture as the crucifixion was; we can easily imagine what his life with the monks will be like.

The Untilled Field and *The Lake* were a preparation for this novel. In fact the landscape of Judea and Galilee in *The Brook Kerith* bears a remarkable similarity to the Irish landscape. 'My life is like these bare hills' says Joseph of Arimathea in his search for Jesus. Even the peasants and the corrupt clerics are familiar.

V

At the beginning of *Hail and Farewell*, after Martyn's declared intention to write in Irish, Moore recalls Turgenev's words: 'Russia can do without any one of us, but none of us can do without Russia' (p. 56). Most of Moore's contemporaries would have sympathised with Turgenev's sentiment, but Moore goes on to say that this is 'utterly untrue of Ireland'. Martyn had aroused something in him that was related to, but different in quality and emphasis from, Martyn's particular vision regarding Ireland. Moore goes on: 'I had heard of Grania for the first time that night, and she might be written about; but not by me, for only what my eye has seen, and my heart felt, interests me' (p. 57).

Moore was looking for something essentially different from any of his contemporaries, all of whom were more interested in, and capable of writing about, Ireland's myths. Synge took the very same people that Moore wrote about, but made them highly colourful, bold and articulate people. Moore was in no way interested in using Ireland as a mythology. His attempt at collaborating with Yeats on a play of *Diarmaid and Grania* was doomed before it began.

'Art must be parochial in the beginning to become cosmopolitan in the end' (p. 56) he says, and this is the very nub of his vision, the goal of his pilgrimage to Ireland. In this context the pilgrimage was an unqualified success. From the parishes of *The Untilled Field* and *The Lake* came the parishes of Judea and Galilee in *The Brook Kerith*. Ireland had helped him forget his cosmopolitan masterpiece.

The best story (and Moore's favourite) in *The Untilled Field* is 'So on He Fares'; along with *The Lake* it features Ireland less as an aspect of psyche than do the other stories. Moore had to struggle to free himself of Ireland as a myth. That he succeeded is a measure of his greatness, and is the most sterling 'model' he could have left to future Irish writers.

GEORGE MOORE'S *THE LAKE*: A POSSIBLE SOURCE[1]

John Cronin

A pamphlet which may be the source of the denouement of *The Lake* has recently been sent to me by Sir Patrick Coghill, literary executor of Somerville and Ross. Sir Patrick found the pamphlet with miscellaneous Somerville and Ross papers and is of the opinion that it may have belonged to Violet Martin. It is entitled 'Rev. T. Connellan to his Dearly Beloved Brethren, the Roman Catholics of the Diocese of Elphin'. The printer is J.T. Drought, 6, Bachelor's Walk, Dublin. The pamphlet is undated and has nine pages, numbered 3 to 11. The author is Thomas Connellan, who describes himself as 'Late Roman Catholic Curate, St. Peter's, Athlone'.

The bulk of Thomas Connellan's message to his former charges consists of an explanation of his reasons for abandoning the Catholic faith and his ministry among them. This is conventional stuff enough and of no great interest now, but the opening of the last paragraph would seem to be of peculiar interest in relation to Moore's novel:

I do not propose to touch upon any more points of controversy just now, but from what I have written, you will gather that it would have been dishonourable and wicked of me to remain in the Church of Rome. Of course the proper thing for me to do was to write to my bishop, and resign into his hands the charge he had given me seven years previously. But you know how a poor Irish priest, who retires from his ministry for conscientious motives, is reviled and persecuted. Then my parents were living. I dare say some of you know them, and if you do, you are aware that they are devout Roman Catholics, and are respected and esteemed by their acquaintances. They doated upon me, and I knew they would much prefer to weep over my dead body than mourn over what to them would be my fall. I gave them the easier alternative. On Tuesday, the 20th of September, 1887, I said Mass in St. Peter's, Athlone, as usual; had a talk with my old parish priest, Dr. Coffey, about schools, after breakfast, and then left, as I suppose for ever. I sent a suit of secular clothes to my boat, pulled up to Lough Ree, and, having left my lay suit on the bank, undressed in the boat and swam ashore. I thank God that from that moment I have had, what I had not tasted for years previously, perfect peace. I got a position as sub-editor on a London newspaper, and for eighteen months gave myself to deep and constant study in the British Museum.[2]

Much of the detail here is reminiscent of that in *The Lake*. Fr. Gogarty swims all the way to freedom while Fr. Connellan uses a boat for part of the journey, but the details in regard to the disposal of the clothing are very similar. Fr. Connellan's conviction that it is impossible for him to continue a priest is echoed in the novel:

> I can imagine nothing more shameful than the life of a man who continues his administrations after he has ceased to believe in them, especially a Catholic priest, so precise and explicit are the Roman Sacraments.[3]

The reasons given for the pretended death by drowning are also similar. Fr. Connellan fears the consequences for his parents, while Fr. Gogarty mentions his sisters in the same connection:

> This way of escape seemed at first fantastic and unreal, but it has come to seem to me the only practical way out of my difficulty. In no other way can I leave the parish without giving pain to the poor people, who have been very good to me. And you, who appreciated my

scruples on this point, will, I am sure, understand the great pain it would give my sisters if I were to leave the Church. It would give them so much pain that I shrink from trying to imagine what it would be. They would look upon themselves as disgraced, and they would think that I have disgraced the whole family. My disappearance from the parish would even do them harm — Eliza's school would suffer. This may seem an exaggeration, but certainly Eliza would never quite get over it. (pp. 272-3)

Fr. Connellan's last chat with his parish priest 'about schools' recalls Fr. Gogarty's involvement with his local school where he encounters Rose Leicester. Finally, Fr. Connellan's journalistic career recalls Fr. Gogarty's forecast:

My life for a long time will be that of some poor clerk or some hack journalist, picking up thirty shillings a week when he is in luck. I imagine myself in a threadbare suit of clothes edging my way along the pavement, nearing a great building, and making my way to my desk, and, when the day's work is done, returning home along the same pavement to a room high up among the rafters, close to the sky, in some cheap quarter. (pp. 279-80)

The possible links all concern points of detail in the plot. Moore's motivation of his story is, of course, entirely his own and unrelated to the rather trivial Scriptural nit-picking in which Fr. Connellan engages in his pamphlet. Oliver Gogarty's penultimate letter to his *femme fatale* makes it perfectly clear that his decision has been fashioned by forces stronger than intellectual or doctrinal considerations:

I might have read the Scriptures again and again, and all the arguments that Mr. Ellis can put forward, without my faith having been shaken in the least. When the brain alone thinks, the thinking is very thin and impoverished. (p. 276)

In his biography of Moore, Joseph Hone indicates that

Moore's denouement for *The Lake* had a source in real life:

> . . . the closing episode — the priest's swim across the
> lake, his old clothes left on the shore, his new awaiting
> him on the other side — had been suggested by an
> incident of real life. There was a Protestant clergyman
> in Dublin, formerly a Roman Catholic priest and at this
> time a conductor of Protestant missions among the poor,
> of whom the same story of escape was told.[4]

Hone does not identify this figure by name but the details of
our pamphlet would seem to suggest that it is indeed Fr.
Thomas Connellan who lies behind Fr. Gogarty and that his
escapade suggested the finale of Moore's celebrated novel.
The *British Museum Catalogue* does not list this pamphlet
but it does list what looks like an Italian version of it.[5] The
date supplied for this (1889) would concur with the information in the passage from the pamphlet quoted above, where
Fr. Connellan indicates that he left his parish in September,
1887, and worked for eighteen months in London. Moore
had originally thought of including *The Lake* among the
stories in *The Untilled Field* (1903). Thus, the pamphlet
would have appeared close to the time when Moore was
preparing the stories for his collection, among them the
story which was to prove too long for that book and was to
appear as a separate novel two years later. Geographically,
too, the connection is clear. Lough Ree, the setting for Fr.
Connellan's 'disappearance', links the counties of Longford,
Westmeath and Roscommon, with the latter bordering on
Moore's home county of Mayo.[6]

THE CONTINUOUS MELODY OF *THE LAKE*

Clive Hart

I

The Lake and the collection of stories called *The Untilled Field*, to which the novel bears a close relationship, were Moore's first substantial literary achievements after his return to Ireland in the spring of 1901. In the 1890s he had been able to write only one wholly successful novel, *Esther Waters*, and his reputation was again in decline. In *The Lake*, for which he always expressed a high regard, he created a new, fresh, simpler manner, mastering a distinctive style which he continued to develop in later work. Although the new novel had only a modest public success, it was clear that in this short book he had once again created something of lasting worth.

By 1904, when most of the first draft of *The Lake* was written, Moore had already lost much of the enthusiasm with which he had returned to Ireland. He had severed his connexion with the Irish Literary Theatre (later the Abbey Theatre) and, following his public renunciation of Catholicism, his anticlerical attitudes, unequivocally expressed in letters to his brother Maurice, were growing more pronounced. Moore set the novel in his own home environment, lightly fictionalizing Lough Carra and the woods and villages around Moore Hall. The priest's flight from dogma reflects Moore's own, while the physical flight from Ireland presages Moore's departure in 1911.

The Lake is simple, almost as simple as a novel may be. Father Oliver Gogarty is seen, initially, to be in ignorance of his own nature and of the true nature of his fellow men. During the year-long process of self-discovery and self-definition he prepares himself for a subsequent period of learning about

other people, other experience, and the novel ends as he
emerges, stripped of prejudice, into life. A rigid form of belief
constrains rather than uplifts the limited and decaying society
to which Oliver belongs by birth but from which he chooses
to sever himself completely. With difficulty he puts aside
dogmatic christianity so that he may embrace a newly discovered secular faith, into which he is baptized by his total
immersion in the lake ('now one of the baptizers had been
baptized'[1]). Rose Leicester, the expelled school-mistress, is
life's prophet, indeed at times almost its goddess. At first she
is, like Christ, directly manifest 'on earth', in Oliver's Ireland.
Later, having been rejected, driven from the temple, morally
crucified, she communicates with Oliver from a distance,
from 'the other world' of European culture, his communion
with her replacing an intermittent and waning communion
with God in which he gradually comes to see only an empty
form. The other world of the scriptures gives way to the
alternative earthly life, the life of the flesh, of the arts, of
temporal beauty, of culture. Moore makes the equation
explicit, sometimes, one may feel, a shade too explicit.
Gogarty identifies culture with anti-Christian attitudes
(p. 212), while in the same context Rose is allowed to
say: 'I am having a heavenly time — yes, indeed, a really
heavenly time' (p. 208). The primitive countryside surrounding Gogarty's home in the west of Ireland physically expresses
the limitations of mortal existence seen in the light of an unsatisfactory form of Christian belief. Oliver learns to sacrifice
the ephemeral world not to the absolute immortality of the
scriptural heaven, but to the relative immortality of secular
human endeavour, both in the arts and in the shaping of a
satisfying pattern for the full enjoyment of human potential
('it seems now to me to be clearly wrong to withhold our
sympathy from any side of life', p. 227). In order to live a
better life, one must be prepared to make the difficult choice
to 'die' and to be reborn, to put aside the former self to
which one has clung and to embrace a new, unknown personality which will emerge out of new experience. While
undergoing a death of the spirit, Oliver also plays out a
physical simulacrum of death, allowing his parishioners to
think that he has been drowned and symbolically leaving his

old self behind on the lake shore with the neatly arranged bundle of clothes which betoken the former inner man. The reborn Oliver, rising naked and in pain from the grey waters of the lake, does not, of course, make his way immediately to the European cultural haven which has been continually offered as the ultimate goal. He goes instead to America, since with his newly acquired simple wisdom he knows that he must first reshape himself; rebirth will be followed by a new period of maturation.

While this is to some degree an anticlerical, anti-Catholic book, and while it explores the need to abandon the sacred in order to enjoy the life-giving profane, it denies neither the value nor the necessity of spiritual experience. Both as priest and as man Oliver is sympathetically drawn, and while he may betray his religion and his country (p. 76) it is a betrayal, by implication, as much for their ultimate benefit as for his own. He does not so much abandon the Christian River as head towards its source where, following Rose, he will experience at first hand 'the great oneness of nature' (p. 253).[2] Confined initially to the 'decrepit dusty house' of Catholicism, as Siegfried was confined in Mime's hut, Oliver frees himself so that he may mix with his fellows 'and maybe blow a horn on the hillside to call comrades together' (p. 254). But throughout the novel Moore implies that in secular life and love true Christian fulfilment may be found.

In the central passages of the book Moore makes new and interesting use of the epistolary form to explore the growth of Oliver's self-awareness and the development of his relationship with Rose. Rose must be physically remote, she must inhabit another world where the rules of life as he knows them in the west of Ireland do not apply, and from which she may educate him. In order to do so she presents him with explicitly literary experience, setting down for him a new Gospel, a new form of the Word, by which he learns to change himself for the better. Rose is also, of course, a developing ideal. Oliver knows very little of her real personality and, as he himself confesses, he does not understand even those things in her which he does know. (Father O'Grady's correspondence begins with unconscious irony: 'I am writing to ask you if you know anything about a young woman called Rose

Leicester', p. 49.) If he were to be confronted with the full reality of 'the other life' and of Rose's part in it, he would be dazzled, would be totally unable to cope. Instead, Rose creates for him a pseudo-self in words, a personality expressly tailored for his needs until, her purpose clearly achieved, she feels free to sever communication and leave him to find his own way.

The epistolary exchange gives Oliver the chance of expressing himself to himself, of creating an external literary model of his own character. His spiritual self had been aroused in his youth — 'His childhood had been a slumber, with occasional awakenings or half awakenings, and Eliza's announcement that she intended to enter the religious life was the first real awakening' (p. 13) — but his physical self remains dormant until, like Siegfried, he learns of the flesh from his Brünnhilde (p. 169). In the end we glimpse the possibility that a fully integrated man may emerge, but in the meantime Oliver is troubled by the split in his being. He is puzzled by his own complexity which at first he does not wish to acknowledge but which he gradually learns to accept as he writes about himself. Before his conversion he takes the absence of self-knowledge for granted ('As if he knew why he hadn't come home to dinner', p. 42), but the distance between his consciousness and his active personality is always a matter of concern: 'His changing mind interested him, and he watched it' (p. 48); 'He noticed with pleasure that he no longer tried to pass behind a thicket nor into one when he met poor wood-gatherers bent under their heavy loads (p. 54). The closing of the gap between observer and observed is among the most significant psychological movements in the book. Not only is Oliver, the observer, shown to be initially remote from physical experience, but the consequent distinction between what he finds sensuously attractive and what morally acceptable is continually emphasized. Rose's appearance is early held to be 'against her' (p. 36), and shortly afterwards Oliver speculates on the relative importance of the visual and the spiritual: 'All night long he had repeated with variations that it were better that all which our eyes see — this earth and the stars that are in being — should perish utterly, be crushed into dust, rather than a mortal sin should be committed' (pp. 39-40). Before his reawakening he treats his own being as similarly observable, sinful, and potentially dispensable. Although when he was writing *The Lake* Moore had moved a long way from his youthful adherence to ideas he had encountered in Paris, he made his priest learn to become, like Gautier, a man 'for whom the visible world is visible'. Salvation for Oliver lies mainly in recognizing the primacy of physical experience.

The attainment of self-knowledge requires, paradoxically, the growth of self-forgetfulness. Although superficially self-castigatory, Oliver's early scrutiny of himself from a distance reveals, in reality, a high degree of unsatisfactory self-involvement. While seeming to be concerned for others, Oliver repeatedly returns to the question of his own spiritual and psychological comfort. 'It would greatly relieve his mind' to know the identity of the father of Rose's baby, and he would be similarly relieved to learn whether she is living in sin with Mr. Ellis. Such prurient curiosity serves to stress the degree of Oliver's covert sexual interest in Rose, but it serves also to stress the degree of his concern for himself. His letters to Father O'Grady displease that kindly old man not only because of their lascivious undertone, but also because of the continual emphasis on their author's own needs.

Oliver's decision to leave and to change his mode of life brings a change of attitude to himself. He enters the new world in a totally unselfconscious way, his observing mind now integrated with his physical, observable being so that, like Joyce's Stephen Dedalus, whose flight to Europe owes something to the priest's example, he is able to cry 'Welcome, O life!' and plunge into its many hazards without concern for his dignity or for the opinions that others will henceforth hold of him.

II

Throughout his career Moore responded strongly and directly to a great many literary and aesthetic influences. Prior to the writ-

ing of *The Lake*, impressionism, naturalism, and Wagnerism
had all been reflected in his work. On his return to Ireland he
began to explore the notion of a fiction rooted in the 'untilled
field' of his native land and, although he was soon to repudiate
many of the ideals of an Irish national literature, *The Lake*
owes much of its excellence and special aesthetic character
to Moore's adoption of an Irish subject. His own knowledge
of the environment and of the psychology of the protagonists
enabled him to work from the inside, to tell the main events
of the story in retrospect and to do so as a natural consequence of Oliver's brooding on his present spiritual state.
The past is treated more as a shaping force in the mind of
the priest, as a set of spiritual circumstances, than as conventional narrative flashback. In doing this Moore was conscious of a struggle against difficulties. As he wrote in the
introduction to the revised edition of 1921: 'The difficulty
overcome is a joy to the artist, for in his conquest over the
material he draws nigh to his idea, and in this book mine was
the essential rather than the daily life of the priest.'

The Lake was something new in Moore's novel-writing.
Information about Oliver's life in Mayo is conveyed not by
Zolaesque detail, not by an accumulation of facts, but by
suggestion, by impressionism. The splendid opening passage,
hazy, colourful, and highly visual, might be compared with
the effect of some impressionist paintings, especially perhaps
those of Monet. Inner and outer coalesce; the visual scene is
directly expressive of Oliver's psychological state, and Moore,
who himself likened the opening to the prelude to *Lohengrin*,
achieves something akin to the fusion of inner experience and
outward form which he prized in Wagner. Although Moore
showed little real understanding of music in general or of
Wagnerian techniques in particular, he succeeded in creating,
in *The Lake*, some interesting fictional parallels with Wagnerian
music drama. There are many leitmotivs of different kinds —
images: roses, the lake; concepts: atonement, rebirth; recurrent
phrases: 'teaching the children the catechism and their A, B,
C', 'relieving one's mind'. There is the celebration of woman
as 'life' (p. 264). And there is the explicit parallel with
Siegfried, including an attempt to create a verbal equivalent
of the 'forest murmurs'. The fluent, harmonious prose of

much of the book is a stylistic equivalent of Wagner's endless melody, while the simple narrative structure bears some relation to that of music drama.

The novel is also notable for its direct, undisguised, but delicately handled symbolism. The fundamental polarities are simple almost to the point of allegory; the colourful, semi-exotic rose, the flesh personified, attracts and binds, while the cold grey lake of the unawakened Irish heart divides. This simple opposition is continuously enriched, modified, developed. The lake, so repeatedly associated with greyness, is occasionally more colourful, more attractive: 'This lake was beautiful, but he was tired of its low gray shores' (p. 6). Sometimes it is directly associated with the inner life of Oliver, sometimes it is no more than a physical barrier. Both the word 'rose' and the more general floral imagery with which Rose Leicester is associated are developed in an endless series of motif transformations. Flowers are of great emotional importance to Oliver. He thinks that they are the only form of beauty available to common men: 'Flowers . . . are the only beautiful things within the reach of these poor people' (p. 87). He himself cultivates carnations, flowers of the flesh, but above all it is of course the rose, symbol of love and passion, which represents the hope of life: 'Roses are happily within the reach of all' (p. 87). Rubens, painter of voluptuous women, had 'rosy' wives. Rose's eyes are grey, a blessed symbolic fusion of the exotic flesh and the spirit of Ireland which recurs in the final moments before Oliver's departure: 'Rose-coloured clouds had just begun to appear midway in the pale sky — a beautiful sky, all gray and rose — and all this babble about baptism seemed strangely incongruous' (p. 288).

The special strength of *The Lake* lies in its delicate combination of warmly evoked daily life in an Irish backwater with a symbolic dimension, of relevance to all men, evolving organically from those mundane materials. The double focus is especially well handled in the fully developed genre piece at the end, the Irish comic story of the double baptism, which develops and strengthens the ambiguous presentation of Oliver's relationship with his society. Here, late in the book, we are given our one extended view of the priest in his role as leader, condemned, it seems, to guide his flock in petty, ludicrous, and fruitless pursuits. He is quite right in his judgement, several times expressed, that these people will for a time be lost without their leader, but both he and the reader learn, in this extended metaphor of childishness, how doubtful is the value of leadership in such a society. The story, placed immediately before the passage about the 'beautiful sky, all grey and rose' signalling the attainment of integration within Oliver's personality, serves as a prelude to his spiritual baptism in the lake of the heart which he is now ready to cross.

III

As with so many of Moore's works, the history of the publication and subsequent revision of *The Lake* is complex. The first edition, which appeared after some delay in November 1905, was rapidly withdrawn when Moore decided that immediate revision was necessary. The so-called 'second impression', also dated November 1905, was in reality a heavily emended text constituting a second edition. (The publisher subsequently issued a spurious 'second impression', consisting of the sheets of the withdrawn first impression of the main text, preceded by the preliminary pages of the true 'second impression'.) The Tauchnitz edition, of 1906, is slightly revised in Chapter XIV, but is otherwise identical in substance to the first edition. The novel was again extensively revised for the edition of 1921, with which those of 1932 and 1936 are identical in substance.

With the exception of a few very minor changes, probably attributable to the printer or the house-editor, the first American edition, of February 1906, which was entirely reset, is identical in substance to the first British edition of 1905.

Of these versions the earliest is plainly the least satisfactory. Rose's letters are too pedantic and far too long (one of them runs to twenty-eight pages), and the reverie through which

Oliver's character is principally revealed is underdeveloped. While in each of the revisions Moore introduced some improvements, and while the version of 1921 is most commonly read, I believe that the first revision (1905) has special merits. Rose was transformed from the garrulous, superficial, and flirtatious bluestocking of the first edition into a mature and sensitive woman who had discovered both life and the arts and who is sufficiently compassionate to devote some time and emotional energy to leading a man whom she once liked and admired into fresh spiritual air. In the final version (1921) Moore reduced Rose's part in the story still more, increasing the attention given to the priest, but rendering Rose (now called Nora) an unsubstantial and uninteresting person whose letters no longer serve as important aids to Oliver's sentimental and cultural education. The world of art and secular experience to which Oliver is converted is much less clearly defined, most of the important analogies with Wagner are abandoned, and the nature of Oliver's growth is made a good deal vaguer. Other major changes in the 1921 edition include the cutting of the priest's dinner scene and the substitution of a highly unlikely visit to Mayo by Father O'Grady. While this substitution contributes superficially to the coherence of the book, it greatly weakens one's understanding of the rural clerical background from which Oliver ultimately escapes, thus making his life seem to have still less connexion with the priestly calling than it had in the economical presentation of the first revision. The character of the correspondence between the priests is changed, and our sense of Oliver's spiritual loneliness is disrupted. In a letter written to Richard Best in 1924, Moore said that 'The Lake . . . never was right until I brought over the priest from London'.[3] Here, as so often, his judgement of his own work seems at fault.

Other significant revisions concern Rose herself, whose name is changed from the English-sounding Rose Leicester to the Irish Nora Glynn. Rose, who is pretty, blond, attractive in the first versions, becomes, in 1921, a less than pretty brown-haired, small-faced girl. The beauty and simplicity of the first revision (1905) with its semi-allegorical use of the name, is replaced by something much more commonplace.

The roses in the story lose most of their significance, and many intense, florid passages in Oliver's reveries are toned to flatness, with an increase, perhaps, of verisimilitude, but a lessening of emotional power. One example will suffice. Oliver's musings after receiving Rose's first letter are changed from 'She didn't know, that was it; nor was there any way of making her understand; that was the worst of it . . . Yet the letter he had written from the convent was plain enough. She must have guessed' (p. 102), to 'And he walked up and down the room, trying to quell the bitterness rising up within him'.

In the first revision of the first edition, Moore blends the narrating voice and that of the priest, creating a highly unified texture akin, on the one hand, to interior monologue and, on the other, to continuous melody. In the later edition Moore frequently used quotation marks and altered phrasing in order to distinguish the priest from the narrator, thus putting the reader at a greater distance and destroying the homogeneity of texture. After a lapse of more than a decade Moore seems to have lost touch with the special qualities of his own book. While in some matters of detail he was able to remove and refine redundancies and clumsy turns of phrase, the 1921 version seems to me to be on the whole less attractive than his sensitive achievement of 1905.

SIEGFRIED IN IRELAND: A STUDY OF MOORE'S
THE LAKE[1]

Max E. Cordonnier

The Lake (1905), Moore's last novel before the late romances,
assuredly marks an important stage in the development of his
once renowned 'melodic line', the quaint dead-end experiment
outside the mainstream of psychological fiction. The author
himself shares the enthusiasm of his stylistic admirers. 'The
drama passes within the priest's soul, it is tied and untied by
the flux and reflux of sentiments, inherent in and proper to
his nature, and the weaving of a story out of the soul substance without ever seeking the aid of external circumstances
seems to me a little triumph.'[2] In a letter to Lady Cunard he
again speaks of its form, calling *The Lake* his 'landscape
book — and some of the landscape is a memory of the forest.
"The forest is like a harp", the breeze lifts the branches and
a bird sings; a touch of art was added to the vague murmur
I hear and the Siegfried music was made'.[3] If his reference to
Wagner reminds us of the origin of 'stream-of-consciousness'
technique,[4] it must be remembered that *The Lake* as well as
Moore's other fiction is highly conventional beside the experi-
ments of his greater contemporaries; the weaving of psychic
and natural landscape through a modified epistolary form is
a conservative venture compared to *Prufrock* or *The Waste
Land, Ulysses* or *Finnegans Wake*.

The real significance of *The Lake* lies not in its stylistic
originality but in its complex embodiment of Moore's human-
ism. Nowhere else in the Moore canon are his values better
represented than in this story of a young priest whose expulsion of a woman for 'illicit behaviour' sets off a long psychological conflict that ends with him casting off his bonds and

embracing 'human' life. A more sophisticated hero than most of his counterparts in the other novels, Father Gogarty verbalizes man's dilemma, as Moore sees it: the question of conscience 'forced him to conclude that there is no moral law except one's own conscience, and the moral obligation of every man is to separate the personal conscience from the impersonal conscience. By the impersonal conscience he meant the opinions of others, traditional beliefs, and the rest' (p. 173). The subtleties of this struggle to realise one's inner moral being (Cf. the two 'consciences' of Huckleberry Finn) are dramatised in his art; he pictures man driven by inner and outer forces, victimised by chance and circumstance, a creature prone to extremes but seeking a precarious balance for a self he cannot prove in a mysterious, uncertain universe. In *The Lake* one also finds the recurrent patterns of Moore's humanistic art: here, as elsewhere, he focuses upon a hero or heroine, typically a sheltered, recluse figure; he lays bare the forces — romantic, religious, sometimes materialistic — that have moulded his conscious values (the impersonal conscience); a confrontation with the world brings latent, repressed desires to the surface, generating a 'soul-struggle' that is eventually resolved. In Father Gogarty of *The Lake*, Esther Waters, Jesus of *The Brook Kerith*, and Alice Barton of *Muslin* we see those who have existentially resisted the depersonalising forces. In other central figures we see the failure to do so; thus Lewis Seymour takes the course of bourgeois materialism, Frank Escott of *Spring Days* is lost hopelessly in Celtic romanticism, Heloise and Abelard in spiritual sterility. None of Moore's heroes totally chooses his own destiny; the sovereign free will has been cast aside, as Father Gogarty's own words imply: 'Volumes have been written on the subject of predestination and freewill, and the truth is that it is as impossible to believe in one as in the other' (p. 159). Thomas Mann's description of Wagner's Siegfried could well apply to the dilemma of Moore's priesthero: 'It is a pregnant complex, gleaming up from the unconscious, of mother-fixation, sexual desire, and fear . . . a complex that displays Wagner the psychologist in remarkable agreement with another typical son of the nineteenth century, the psychoanalyst Sigmund Freud.'[5] While Moore eschews both Wagner's romanticism and Freud's determinism, any discussion of *The Lake* must probe that gleaming complex of Fr. Gogarty. In the depths of his crisis, the priest's dream recalls the death of Siegfried: 'He began to dream of a hunt, the quarry hearing with dying ears the horns calling to each other in the distance, and cast himself in his chair, his arms hanging like dead arms' (p. 119). To describe closely Fr. Gogarty's struggle, descent, and emergence into relative freedom is to learn much about Moore's view of man; Bayreuth and Dujardin touched not only his literary methods but his *Weltanschauung*. In 1897 he wrote to the French editor of the *Revue Wagnerienne* about the new style of *Les Lauriers sont coupés*. Dujardin recalls that: 'il me disait que j'avais trouvé la forme la plus originale de notres temps, mais que la psychologie etait un peu naturalist.'[6] Our concern in *The Lake* is just what goes on in the priest's soul.

Moore's claim for a psychological drama independent of external circumstances does not really mark a striking departure from his earlier fiction. All his novels are psychological. The differences are simply that the catalyst in Fr. Gogarty's soul-change (the expulsion of Nora Glynn) is already at work when the novel begins and that overt action is subordinated to reflection; but here, as in the other novels, the impersonal conscience is soon delineated. While the complexity of the forces which shape his conflict may well support Moore's claim for a special depth of treatment in *The Lake*, one initially encounters the familiar blend of ascetic and romantic values in his hero: Fr. Gogarty had spent much of his childhood in a small, oppressive shop owned by his parents; his antipathy toward marriage is grounded in the threat that it will perpetuate the 'shop' existence which he 'instinctively' loathes, intellectually and physically. His asceticism, both self-imposed and circumstantial, reinforces his romantic tendencies: he dreams of running a great engineering project to rebuild the mills in his hometown and restore them to commercial prosperity. It is a short step from his romantic books about robbers and pirates to the passion he develops when his favorite sister Eliza, whom he idolizes with latent sexual fervour, decides to take the veil. Though Eliza supposes that 'his interest in hermits sprang from a boyish taste for adventure rather than religious feeling', Gogarty is actually carried ever deeper into other-worldly excess.

At college, even the president is distressed by his more than steadfast piety; he grows ashamed of his own intellectual prowess and puts pebbles in his shoes to punish himself and keeps 'a cat-o'-nine-tails in his room, and scourged himself at night' (p. 12). One day he bares his back to a fellow student: 'with a gentle smile he handed the whip to Tom Bryan, the very smile which he imagined the hermits of old time used to wear' (p. 13). By the time he leaves college, Gogarty has a fully developed impersonal conscience, making him scorn his intellectual powers and sink to a self-torture and self-denial fraught with masochistic tendencies and latent sexual desires.

In the beginning the parish priest firmly holds the values of his youth, yet already his pious act of banishment has begun to generate discord. Now the conflict is subdued because he cannot consciously scrutinise its hidden causes, which range from inhibited sexual desire (with its jealousy when Nora Glynn was 'unfaithful' to him) to a deeper impulse to break the bonds of the impersonal conscience. His early wandering thoughts, however, foreshadow his ultimate divorce from Ireland. He ponders the mysterious, alien life of trees, objects of ancient worship so different from a personal deity; he recalls the brutality of nature when he and his brother had taken home a nest of young hawks who ate one another even though they were well fed. His reactions toward a nest of ducklings reflect his latent desires for freedom: 'many of the ducklings had broken their shells; these struggled after the duck; but there were two prisoners, two that could not escape from their shells, and seeing their lives would be lost if he did not come to their aid, he picked the shells away and took them to the water's edge' (pp. 37-8). But Fr. Gogarty's thoughts are intermingled with romantic fantasy that keeps his conflict subdued; his desire to disavow this asceticism and love a woman can only take the shape of day-dream: 'A sailor might draw a pinnace alongside, and he imagined a woman being helped into it and rowed to the landing-place' (p. 38). He can think of the nuns as being estranged from the world, ignores the legends of brutality and vengeance of the old Welsh tribesmen who settled in Mayo, and clings nostalgically to thoughts of the monasteries of ancient Ireland.

All his thoughts, of course, are either directly or indirectly related to Nora Glynn. He is never to see her again, but in his changing image of her and of their relationship can be seen the process of self-discovery. With his typical psychological realism, Moore fashions no sudden breaks or reversals; each stage of the process dynamically coalesces with the next. In the beginning the priest interprets his anguish over the banishment in rigid, traditional terms; he feels his responsibility in losing a soul from the fold. When he first writes to Nora about coming back for a convent job, he speculates how unpleasant 'it must be to a Catholic to live in a Protestant country'. When he learns that Nora is working for Fr. O'Grady in London, he feels that God had sent her to safety, but her becoming the secretary of the sceptical writer Walter Poole is a blatant act of her own wilfulness. Fr. Gogarty is far from understanding Nora's own resolution to pursue her studies regardless of conclusions; he has barely cracked his shell. Walter Poole offers the first serious intellectual challenge to his beliefs; living in his spacious eighteenth-century hall, charming, unaffected, reserved, writing not for the many but the few, he becomes Moore's spokesman, much as the novelist Harding was in previous works:

> If, for instance, Mr. Walter Poole is asked if he be al-together sure that it is wise to disturb people in their belief in the traditions and symbols that have held sway for centuries, he will answer quickly that if truth lies behind the symbols and traditions, it will be in the interest of the symbols and traditions to enquire out the truth, for blind belief — in other words, faith — is hardly a merit, or if it be a merit it is a merit that cannot be denied to the savages who adore idols. (p. 87)

In his weak answer to Nora Glynn's increasing scepticism under Poole's influence, Fr. Gogarty says that he himself is not qualified to answer all problems about belief, but that the Catholic Church has an answer for all the charges against its dogma. Yet, for all his intellectual affinities with his creator, Mr. Poole is stagnant beside the dynamic source of love and beauty represented by Nora Glynn. Moore continually says that our knowledge alone cannot save us, and the sceptical researcher among the old scrolls has abstracted himself from life in another direction. The breakdown of dogmatic belief in itself is insufficient; along with Yeats, Moore believed that we can embody truth but cannot know it, and that embodiment must be like a great-rooted blossomer, a dancer in the dance. Not until the end of *The Lake* will Fr. Gogarty wholly understand the meaning of Nora Glynn. She will then be 'like a fountain, shedding living water' upon his life: 'A fountain springs out of earth into air; it sings a tune that cannot be caught and written down in notes; and rising and falling water is full of iridescent colour, and to the wilting roses the fountain must seem not a natural thing, but a spirit, and I too think of her as a spirit' (p. 135).

Fr. Gogarty develops by subtle half-steps. In a long series of dramatically ironic letters to Nora Glynn, he unwittingly reveals the changes in himself. He writes cautioning Nora that her indifference may pass 'into unbelief, and you will write to me (if we continue to write to each other) in such a way that I shall understand that you have come to regard our holy religion as a tale fit only for childhood's ears' (p. 91). In her letters to him, the priest discerns three different Noras — the Nora with intellectual interests, the Nora as a possible mistress, and the Nora who is too spontaneous and alive for the arid studies of Mr. Poole. These three images, of course, correspond respectively to his own desires to throw off the dogmatic knowledge of Catholicism, to become sexually involved in a way his ascetic conscience had never allowed, and generally to commit himself to the personal conscience, the wellspring of his own nature. His own beliefs are binding; midway through the novel he still sees his own struggle and Nora's in traditional terms: 'There is ever a divorce between the world of sense and the world of spirit, and the question of how much love we may expend upon external things will always arise, and will always be a cause of perplexity to those who do not choose to abandon themselves to the general drift of sensual life' (p. 99).

Every detail of the priest's soul-struggle need not be glossed here; when Moore wrote to Dujardin that *Les Lauriers sont coupés* showed 'la petite vie de l'ame devoilee pour la premiere fois . . . seulement je crains la monotonie',/ his remarks reflect a weakness in his own fiction. Lacking Joyce's brilliant texture or Lawrence's dark lyricism, with a mind prone to common-sense realism, and dedicated to eschewing both melodrama and comedy in his fiction, Moore often falls into dullness and repetition. Thus in letter after letter Fr. Gogarty vacillates from one extreme to another. At one time he is elated over writing a romantic history of the lake to prove religion is not so dry and austere as Mr. Poole makes it; at another he shows disgust with the Sacraments and other once-cherished rituals of the Church; still again, occasionally in the midst of his attempted religious dedication, scenes of the lake and its surroundings well up into his mind as hints of the wholeness of life he has not yet found, as when the lake was 'shrouded in mist, with ducks talking softly in the reeds, and swallows high up, advancing in groups like dancers on a background of dappled clouds' (p. 92). From such images of unity and freedom he sometimes sinks into void and depression:

Yesterday I went for a long walk in the woods, and I can find no words that would convey an idea of the stillness. It is easy to speak of a tomb, but it was more than that. The dead are dead, and somnambulism is more mysterious than death. The season seemed to stand on the edge of a precipice, will-less, like a sleepwalker . . . The branches dropped, and the leaves hung out at the end of long stems. One could not help pitying the trees, though one knew one's pity was vain. (p. 102)

In short, what one sees are the latent inner desires and values finally standing side by side with impersonal conscience, approximating to Freud's view of the mind: 'the mind is an arena, a sort of tumbling-ground, for the struggles of antagonistic impulses; or, to express it in non-dynamic terms, . . . the mind is made up of contradictions and pairs of opposites. Evidence of one particular tendency does not in the least preclude its opposite; there is room for both of them.'[8]

When his thrust towards freedom is thwarted by his religious values, the priest suffers his most intense conflict; like other ascetics in Moore's fiction, he reaches the stage of delirium, nightmare, and hallucination.[9] Nowhere does the landscape in *The Lake* so well reflect his psychic state as in his search for Nora: he was 'looking for her soul, for her lost soul, and . . . something had told him he would find the soul he was seeking in the wood; so he was drawn from glade to glade through the underwoods, and through places so thickly overgrown that it seemed impossible to pass through' (p. 115). His divided mind, welling with desire but censored by the impersonal conscience, manifests itself in his delirious journey: 'Once he was within the wood, the mist seemed to incorporate again; she descended again into his arms, and this time he would have lifted the veil and looked into her face, but she seemed to forbid him to recognise her under penalty of loss' (p. 115). In his dream state he would escape with her to the thick, enclosed wood, but his visionary Nora says he must abide by the lake; he has reached a point at which a kind of love-in-death retreat seems the only answer. Thomas Mann says of Wagner's heroines, a subject fresh in Moore's mind after *Evelyn Innes*, that 'they have something sleepwalking, ecstatic, and prophetic which imparts an odd, uncanny modernity to their romantic heroics'[10]; like a more realistic Siegfried, Fr. Gogarty must free himself of the 'gods' and forge a human life.

While the lake itself seems an insufferable barrier to his dogma-ridden self, it takes on broad spiritual overtones of baptism and rebirth when Fr. Gogarty finally answers that 'mysterious warble, soft as lake water, that abides in the heart' (p. x). By slow degrees he sheds his impersonal conscience: first, he must endure the utter loneliness akin to Carlyle's Everlasting Nay or Camus's stage of moral disintegration. He finds that the autumn 'seems to steal all one's courage away, and one looks up from one's work in despair, asking of what value is one's life. The world goes on just the same, grinding our souls away. Nobody seems to care; nothing seems to make any difference' (p. 122). We see him pathetically and ironically calling out to God for Nora's body as well as her soul; he starts to question his duty, but fears the abyss of relativism; his romanticism, his masochism does not die easily, for he imagines Nora as 'some supernatural being whom he had offended, and who had revenged herself. Her wickedness became in his eyes an added grace, and from the rack on which he lay he admired his executioner' (p. 125). The eventually enlightened priest, however, achieves maturity and stability.

He comes to believe that many of man's beliefs and institutions are but shields to protect him from an uncomfortable, complex universe. If Nature has a pattern, it is inscrutable to our eyes; both the great outer world and the inner life are indefinable: 'one never gets at the root of one's nature' and the spontaneous overflow of life cannot be 'written down in notes' (p. 172) as Fr. Gogarty phrases it.

Faced with a world which does not submit to such large inferences about free will or determinism, since either extreme falsifies experience, Moore's hero comes to feel like a decrepit house with sagging roof and lichen-covered walls whose shutters are now falling to let in the splendid sun; he must cut off the dead flesh of tradition and cultivate himself, searching the mysterious depths of the personal conscience:

> He seemed to himself a much more real person than he was a year ago, being now in full possession of his soul, and surely the possession of one's soul is a great reality. By the soul he meant a special way of feeling and seeing. But the soul is more than that — it is a light; and this inner light, faint at first, had not been blown out. If he had blown it out, as many priests had done, he would not have experienced any qualms of conscience. (p. 172)

Although Fr. Gogarty virtually succeeds in fulfilling that 'moral obligation of every man . . . to separate the personal conscience from the impersonal conscience. . .' — now realising that 'body and mind were the same. . .' — the ending of *The Lake* is a tribute to Moore's complex, undogmatic art. The priest can now see that what he had been following was not really Nora, but an abstraction called life; he knows that he could end up with the same habitual frame of mind under a different guise, 'flying from the monotony of tradition' to find only 'another monotony, and a worse one — that of adventure' (p. 175). He also knows that belief is not enough and that he must concentrate on going to New York to earn a living; even in the high seriousness of his setting forth, Fr. Gogarty, like his creator, felt the potential comedy of his venture. There is no end to the striving and 'the bourne (can) never be reached'. Were he to stay, he might well lapse into the old asceticism; now he may become ensnared by new fixed habits and beliefs in the future. Rather than of adventure, he 'liked better to think that his quest was the personal life — the intimate exaltation that comes to him who has striven to be himself, and nothing but himself' (p. 175). With these words another Irish rebel sheds the garments of family, Church and country, seeking that harmony of the 'two rhythms out of which the music of life is made, intimacy and adventure', and Nora, who was now 'an adventure, would become in the end the home of his affections' (p. 177).

If we look deeply into *The Lake*, we can see a radiating image of Moore's art as a whole; nowhere was he more explicit about his values. And, if we look into Fr. Gogarty's soul, we can see the perpetual dilemma of all his heroes and heroines. Wagner's *Ring Cycle* figures significantly in the two works that frame *The Lake* in the Moore canon. Evelyn Innes (Brünnhilde) is driven by her ascetic father (Wotan) to the psychotic state that we find in *Sister Teresa* (1901): 'One night in her convent bed she saw flames about her, and she began to remember the scene — how it begins with Siegfried's own motive, and underneath it the ripple of the Rhinegold.'[11] So lingering is the battle against the impersonal conscience that Evelyn only learns to live a full life after she has sacrificed her youthful years. In *Hail and Farewell* (1911-1914) George Moore again used Wagner's musical epic in both structure and symbolism. Like Fr. Gogarty at the end of *The Lake*, he sees hope in the personal conscience: 'Ireland has lain too long under the spell of the magicians, without will, without intellect, useless and shameful, the despised of nations. I have come into the most impersonal country in the world to preach personality — personal love and personal religion, personal art, personality for all except for God.'[12] In his fantasy he fashions Irish history in terms of *The Ring*: he remembers 'that many had striven to draw forth the sword that Wotan had struck into the tree about which Hunding had built his hut. Parnell, like Sigmund, had drawn it forth, but Wotan had allowed Hunding to strike him with his spear. And the allegory becoming clearer I asked myself if I were Siegfried, son of Sigmund slain by Hunding, and if it were my fate to reforge the sword that lay broken in halves in Mimi's cave.' But Moore, like Fr. Gogarty and other Irish rebels, finds that the *Götterdammerung* is not at hand and must say to his beloved homeland: 'Atque in Perpetuum, Mater, Ave Atque Vale'.

FATHER BOVARY

Joseph Stephen O'Leary

I
The Lake and the tradition of the novel

Let Fielding, Goethe, Stendhal stand for the period in which the novel thrived on the interplay of two interests: the education or quest of the individual protagonist and the exploration and criticism of society. In a novel of this period faith in the individual and faith in society are still intact, despite the tensions between them, and this faith gives the novel the status of a wise and authoritative guide to worldly reality. In the great post-Romantic novels of disillusion, however, (*Illusions perdues, Middlemarch, L'Education sentimentale, Great Expectations*), the self and the world no longer seem so well-matched. The world is a cruel machine crushing the aspirations of the self and the novelist is the one who unveils the horrific laws of the mechanism. Thus Balzac relentlessly analyses the 'capitalization of the spirit';[1] Flaubert convinces us that the social life of Paris and the provinces is a mediocre void; the Dickensian phantasmagoria testifies to a similar emptiness; Zola finally attempts to reduce the workings of society to a positivist formula leaving only illusory spaces for the spirit to breathe. Hillis Miller's account of the nineteenth century 'doubt of the possibility of ever finding the proper form of life'[2] is confirmed by this reduction of social reality to the status of a hostile machine.

The protagonist of these novels is typically Romantic and his or her Romanticism is typically impotent, resigned or self-destructive. But at a certain point a reversal comes to pass in the fortunes of the Romantic subject, a reversal which may be loosely associated with the immense impact of Wagner and Nietzsche on the whole of literary Europe. Already in

Flaubert and Zola the void in society is compensated for by an intense investment in subjective impression and sensation. The novelist ceases for the first time to be primarily a story-teller and sees himself as a stylist, a painter, a musician. Zola paints with relish the succulent meatstuffs in *Le centre de Paris*, and Moore too, in his early Zolaesque period, is more a painter of society than its narrational explorer (since faith that there was anything to explore had declined). Esther Waters triumphs over the monotonous oppressions of society by producing a baby, who appears on the last page as a splendid young man, and this can be read as a Romantic and subjective triumph over the world at large, albeit in the refreshingly wholesome guise of motherly love. The fatal machine grinds on, but life wells up despite it, beyond it. James and Proust maintain a passionate interest in the workings of society, but only as they nourish the develop-ment of a refined aesthetic consciousness — society exists to be consumed in consciousness, consciousness to be trans-formed into style, style to cement the edifice of an imaginary universe, *tout, au monde existe pour aboutir à un livre.*[3]

The Lake celebrates the triumph of the subject in a manner not as cerebral and aesthetic as that of the writers just mentioned. It belongs to a line of novels in which interest in the workings of society is almost eclipsed by the concern to communicate in all its primitive vigour a message of self-realisation, a gospel of Life. Gospels rather than novels are the typical produce of this generation, steeped in Nietzsche's *Zarathustra*, the daunting model of the genre. Whatever ironic distance the evangelist maintains towards his Christ-figure, the novels of Gide, Forster, Lawrence and Joyce's *Portrait* remain stirring affirmations of the self and of life which wrench the novel form away from its traditional social bear-ings. (Others will explore the existential alienation and the fragmentation of identity implicit in this proud isolation of self. In the springtime of their optimism these evangelists show little consciousness of it.) The choices of Moore's priest, Gide's immoralist, Joyce's artist, Lawrences's lovers bear a purely negative, anarchic, relation to a social context, despite dreams of social regeneration. The novel is no longer a *vade mecum* of social wisdom, but a vehicle of utopian unrest, preaching a fulfilment society has failed to provide. Madame Bovary is no longer crushed by the world. Her reinforced rebellious subjectivity, now backed by the collusion of the artist, subverts the established order.

Moore is more Wagnerian than Nietzchean, in that his conception of Life consists more in an opening up to Nature and Love than in the Promethean assumption of one's own destiny as something original, unique and self-created. Moore's priest is portrayed as journeying back to normality where Joyce's Daedalus aspires to a creative abnormality; Father Gogarty defrocks himself in the end, whereas Stephen robes himself as a priest of art. Moore's quest is for the native harmonies of the soul, stifled by the conventional conscience, and so his art is obliged to 'aspire to the condition of music'. But Joyce, more radically, aims at an 'uncreated conscience' and is impelled to do more serious violence to inherited forms.

II
The musical structure of *The Lake*

A certain drabness characterises the 1905 versions of *The Lake* insofar as Moore attempts to give Father Gogarty's self-realisation objective social correlatives. Through Rose Leicester's letters he learns to know the great world and becomes involved, at a distance, in the novelistic plot constituted by her adventures abroad. But in the 1921 version (five years after Joyce's *Portrait*) Rose Leicester (now Nora Glynn) dissolves into a presence as vague as the rose-coloured clouds which are her symbol. The priest's dialogue is with the lake and the wood — the lake calling forth the responses of his heart, varying shades of joy or sadness, the wood nourishing his mind with a deepening sense of the complexity and mystery of life.[4] If, within the space of a year, the priest moves from emotional and intellectual dormancy to a mature and autonomous decision for life, this is not the effect of contact with the world, but of the constant persuasive murmur of lake and forest, summoning the sleeping self to consciousness. The drama, as Moore insists in the 1921 preface, passes within the priest's soul. And paradoxically the other characters are more convincing, now that they are reduced to the function of agents and stimuli of Gogarty's self-realisation, than they were when Moore tried to present them in their full social reality. This is because the narcissistic orbit of Father Gogarty's quest clashed with the residue of conventional narrative in the early versions. In the 1921 version Moore espouses more faithfully the limits of his theme, lets the objective world recede, and brings the form and texture of the novel into harmony with the psychic processes which constitute its real plot.

It is paradoxical too that in the 1921 version Moore has more successfully distanced the priest's quest — we have less the impression that we are being preached at, that we are being asked to participate in a fantasy of wish-fulfilment. This is mainly because Rose Leicester no longer rushes to fulfil the priest's longings — her silence allows the priest's quest to develop with all its tensions, bewilderment and solitude, instead of smothering it with gratuitous commentary. Thus, though the novel is more intensely concentrated on the priest, the sharper definition of his situation creates a satis- fying fictional distance. The tensions and ambiguities in the priest's soul, no longer smoothed over by too helpful voices telling us and him what to think, provide the co-efficient of friction which the objective world provided in the traditional novel. In the 1921 version a silence persists, right to the end of the novel, the silence of the lake's undeciphered enigma. Moore knows now that this silence is the heart of the novel, that the message of self-fulfilment is secondary to the grow- ing sense of mystery the priest's experiences bring, and so he treats much more lightly and discreetly the themes that were so important in 1905, in order to convey in its purity the elusive poetic essence of the novel.

These improvements are reflected in the texture of the 1921 version, which is far more genuinely musical than in 1905; now there are no lectures on Wagner, and the crude labelling of motifs (e.g. those associated with Rose's name) is avoided. Instead the motifs are left to speak for themselves, in their varying degrees of opacity, just as in Wagner. Moore no longer has any desire to attach a message to the priest's experience, realising that it is enough to have evoked the murmur of the heart's discontent. The rhythm of the narrative is more closely attuned to the *impulses* which constitute the principal material of the priest's psychic life, the wavelets on its surface. Indeed Gogarty's character is delightfully suited to the theme of the novel. He is a man of reveries (at several points in the story he falls into a distracted trance), timid, superstitious, his mind easily played upon by thoughts and fancies — 'thoughts are rising up in my mind'; 'I am, as it were, propelled to my writing-table.'[5] When we meet him all his movements betray 'his desire . . . to be freed for a while from everything he had ever seen and from everything he had ever heard' (p. 4) and his soul remains as changeable as the landscape right through the novel even up to his final escape.

The direct expression of feeling in this novel attains a limpidity which again and again really does seem to convey 'the essential rather than the daily life of the priest' (p. x). This is because the melodic line gives the simple diction a musical tone (in the absence of all sophisticated chords, i.e. complex psychological observations) that makes it seem to come from the heart: 'Loneliness begets sleeplessness, and sleeplessness begets a sort of madness. I suffer from nightmare' (p. 93). But the transparency of this language is supported by the opacity of the motifs — these are like a cloudy piano accompaniment lending subtlety to a song in which the vocal line is naive.

While readers have been enchanted by the motival texture of *The Lake* it may be that they have overlooked the musical effects created by the formal structure of the novel, which seems to bear a resemblance to sonata form. One may regard the first four chapters as an exposition section to which the last four chapters correspond. The intervening development comprises three phases: the trip around the lake (chapters five and six); Father O'Grady (chapter seven); and Father Gogarty's agonized winter (chapters eight to ten). It seems important to take account of this structure in order to appreciate the admirable spacing and timing of the changes in the priest's soul. The structure also lends their full significance to the motifs, which often have a structural function as well as a psychological and narrative one. For instance, it is towards the end of the exposition that Gogarty murmurs to himself: 'Every man . . . has a lake in his heart' (p. 35). The completion of his thought comes at the structurally corresponding place at the end of the novel. Again, towards the end of the exposition Gogarty releases ducklings into the water, which corresponds to his own swim to freedom at the novel's end.

The yacht which appears in the exposition (and thereafter vanishes) stimulates the priest's dreams of escape and is linked with the images (from *Siegfried*) of the birdsong and the forest breezes. But just as in *Siegfried* the song of the bird has to be interpreted by the hero, so Father Gogarty is occupied in interpreting the signs that surround him all through the book. The yacht is one of many symbols of a nameless longing. To label it the Nameless Longing motif would however be as preposterous as the musicological practice of labelling even the most elusive of Wagner's motifs. Most of the motifs retain their opacity in Moore's novel even though the priest's soul grows into kinship with the message they convey to him.

The yacht illustrates the musical handling of motifs rather well. At the transition from the first theme of the exposition (Father Gogarty's soul) to the second (Nora Glynn), at the start of the second chapter, the chief motifs of Gogarty's restlessness are recapitulated: 'A breeze rose, the forest murmured, a bird sang, and the sails of the yacht filled' (p. 15). The yacht recurs at the end of the chapter (and at the end of the exposition of the second theme) on page 25. Finally it returns at the very end of the exposition on page 38. The animal dartings in the undergrowth — the fox on page 2 for example — are associated perhaps with the stirrings of life in Father Gogarty; these too recur at the end of the exposition — the rabbit and weasel on page 38. The duckling he releases recalls the ducks warbling in the opening paragraph of the novel. The twilight scene which closes the exposition of the Nora Glynn theme at the end of the second chapter is transformed into a dawn scene at the end of chapter four (reflecting his ecstasy at Nora's forgiveness): 'Rose-coloured clouds descended, revealing many new and beautiful mountain forms, every pass and every crest distinguishable' (p. 25); 'At last a red ball appeared behind a reddish cloud; its colour changed to the colour of flame, paled again, and at four flared up like a rose-coloured balloon' (p. 37). The end of the exposition thus prefigures the happy conclusion of Father Gogarty's travail: 'life emerges like the world at daybreak' (p. 144).[6]

At the start of the recapitulation, in chapter eleven, the Nora Glynn theme re-appears as Gogarty receives her letter, breaking a long silence, on the very anniversary of the opening scene. The lake seen through the priest's eyes may be intended to register an advance from the indeterminacy of that scene: 'more blue in the sky, less mist upon the water' (p. 135). The twilight, when it recurs, is again a moment of clarity and splendour, imaging goddesses around a celestial lake; but, that vision gone, vagueness enshrouds the terrestrial lake again: 'And he watched the earth and sky enfolded in one tender harmony of rose and blue — blue fading to grey, and the lake afloat amid vague shores, receding like a dream through sleep' (p. 139). Chapter twelve is the corresponding recapitulation of the Gogarty theme, taking the form of a letter in reply to hers. He goes over the story of his vocation for the third time in the novel: the first time, in chapter one, it was presented at its face value; in the dialogue with Father O'Grady in chapter seven the ambiguities first emerge into consciousness; here, finally, the true perspective is established, the authentic vocation emerges from behind the false one. The animals of the exposition section come back into the picture (all has been dead in the preceding chapters) as he writes of 'the bleat of the lamb and the impatient cawing of the rook' (p. 144).

III
'Within the priest's soul'

Structurally the 1921 version is a great improvement on both the 1905 versions, an improvement reflecting Moore's closer attention to the essential subject of the novel. In the second 1905 version there is a passage in which Gogarty's fellow-clergy discuss, with much coarseness and narrow-mindedness, his action in denouncing Rose Leicester from the pulpit. This piece of anti-clerical satire is a regression to the 'Protestant' Moore's public critique of Catholicism; it impedes his effort to map the private obstacles Father Gogarty must overcome, obstacles whose personal, inward shape must be allowed to come to light in the course of his lakeside broodings. In the 1921 version it is Father O'Grady who drops in at this point, although it is only five days since he has written to Gogarty from London without giving any warning of a visit to Ireland. Despite this unlikelihood O'Grady's visit gives the story a backbone which is missing in the earlier versions. Rose Leicester's gushing correspondence is also drastically reduced. Her sourvenirs of Bayreuth are no longer supposed to influence the process of Gogarty's liberation in any way, nor is there any attempt to parallel his growth with her own discovery of a bigger world. Wagner was no longer a 'cause' in 1921 nor was Bayreuth the only temple of his genius. (Shaw, in a late foreword to *The Perfect Wagnerite*, indicates that better performances could be attended in London at this time.) The Bayreuth material had in any case been re-used in a charming, comic vein in *Ave* (1911). However, another genius had appeared on the scene and it may be that the O'Grady scene owes something to Freud.

The unlikelihood of Father O'Grady's visit is finely integrated into the texture of the novel by the long evocation of the unease with which both men are smitten, an unease which on Gogarty's part shows his fear of the painful probings to which the encounter exposes him. The scene could seem predictable and melodramatic to a cursory reader; closer reading shows it to be a study of considerable psychological finesse. The apparent melodrama of Gogarty's cry: 'I'm frightened, frightened, my fear is great and at this moment I feel like a man on his deathbed . . . Can I be forgiven if that soul be lost to God?' (p. 81) and of the absolution administered by Father O'Grady, disappears when one realises that Gogarty's cry is an amalgam of several displacements or self-deceptions. His fear is not really fear of divine judgement but of the

moment of truth which is facing him, the immanent judgement of his growth in self-awareness; he is on his deathbed in
the sense that his clerical persona can no longer provide him
with a satisfactory identity; his obsession with Nora's soul is
of a personal and erotic nature, the cultural shield of clerical
convictions preventing it from finding correct expression as
yet. His confession serves the purpose of opening him up to
the real nature of his anxiety. At the moment of absolution
he rejoins the life of instinct in an undistorted form: 'conscious
of the green grass showing through the window, lighted by a
last ray of the setting sun' (p. 81) and is more ready for the
real confession which ensues. 'What had he confessed? Already
he had forgotten.' He asks O'Grady a question which touches
a deeper level: 'if he discovered any other influence except
an intellectual influence in Mr. Poole'; and complains that he
'might have warned Nora of the danger' (this is the first time
in the interview that Gogarty allows himself to call her 'Nora'
rather than 'Miss Glynn'). O'Grady puts two leading questions
'as if he wished to change the subject': 'Tell me how it all
came about'; and 'Was no attempt . . . made to marry you to
some girl with a big fortune?' Gogarty then begins to talk
with growing self-awareness. He is 'a little dazed and troubled
in his mind'; 'he rambled on, telling his story almost unconsciously'; he 'continued, like one talking to himself'. Father
O'Grady, catalyst of this emergence of truth, listens, 'seriously
moved by the story' (that is meant to ward off the reader's
temptation to a slight scorn for Gogarty's confusions), almost
murmurs, 'Now, I'm beginning to understand' and finally
leaves, without comment, 'as if he felt that the object of his
visit had been accomplished'. So it has. 'He goes as a dream
goes', thinks Gogarty, 'Why did he come here? And he was
surprised that he could find no answer to any of the questions
that he put to himself' (p. 84). O'Grady's visit has brought
about a state of lucidity and of crisis — the desolation of the
opening words of the following chapter: 'Nothing will happen
again in my life — nothing of any interest', and the inner
storm matched by an outer one which he describes in his
letter to Nora. The first words of her reply helpfully confirm
that he is on the right path: 'You are a very human person
after all' (p. 97).

The culturally deflected interpretation of his inner turmoil which ensnares Father Gogarty for so long, his difficulty in thinking his way out of his ready-made clerical categories, is handled by Moore with remarkable empathy, and the paradoxical conversion of those categories in the final scene is a convincing resolution of the priest's struggle towards self-understanding. There the lake provides the true equivalent of the baptism over whose external forms a bizarre wrangle between Catholic and Protestant peasants had earlier developed and the rocks become a natural altar on which Gogarty sacrifices his dead clerical identity. Joyce laughed at the dimpled buttocks and earmarked the scene as a comic mythology for use in *Finnegans Wake*. But the comic touch is not unintentional; Moore will not let his priest keep up a dignified sacerdotal air and take his new sacraments more seriously than the old, for the serious theme of his novel is what passes within the soul, and its external enactment is better left as muddled and tragicomical as ordinary life will have it. The combination of this external comedy with the sober chronicle of inner states, in which neither is over-emphasised at the other's expense, is a fine achievement, possible only to one with a long schooling in the bitter-sweet art of Maupassant or Turgenev.

IV
Moore and the Catholic priesthood

Mary McCarthy claims that *Madame Bovary* is the novel that best speaks to the condition of modern American women. If I may add another extra-literary claim, which may not be without literary relevance after all, I would suggest that *The Lake* is the novel that best speaks to the condition of the contemporary Catholic clergyman, insofar as that condition is one of discontent, and that recent history has verified the psychological finesse of Moore's portrait to a surprising extent. Of course there is another dimension, which Moore and Father Gogarty but distantly recognise. That is the dimension of grace, the quest for the essence of the Gospel, sublimely, perhaps too sublimely, expressed in Bernanos' *Journal d'un curé de campagne*. But I cannot think of any novel which evokes as subtly and as exactly as Moore's does the oppressive aspects of a clericalist culture and the psychology of a revolt of which most priests will have some idea, however they resolve the resultant tensions. What distinguishes Moore's treatment from such crude attempts as Zola's *La faute de l'abbe Mouret* is an affectionate feeling for the life of the Irish presbytery and convent. The pathos of *The Lake* is that of revolt against an environment which has claims on the heart. The priest's choice for life on larger terms thus has a boldness and tension to it which it would not have were it merely a matter of fleeing a detestable prison. Again and again good reasons for staying in the rut present themselves, and subtle discernment is needed to overcome this false conscience and strive onward to self-realisation. The indecisive and wavering temperament of Gogarty adds to the interest and subtlety of the drama. Father Gogarty has to tear himself away. Had Moore introduced a more tragic clash of duties, in the manner, for instance, of *Anna Karenin*, his novel might have been greater, a novel of adulthood rather than of late adolescence. But the lack of that dimension too takes nothing from the truth of the novel. Indeed, in presenting the priest, like the hero of 'So on He Fares', as a psychological orphan torn between two mothers, Eliza and Nora, the Church and Nature, Moore may have sensed an aspect of the drama of the Catholic priesthood which has more sociological weight than might appear.

Contemporaries of Moore in Ireland queried the verisimilitude of his clerical portrait, but perhaps for reasons similar to those that caused people to shudder at Flaubert's 'moeurs de province'. Stephen Gwynn, for instance, in *Irish Literature and Drama* (1936), assured us that 'an Irish reader, though well aware that many an Irish priest has succumbed to sexual temptation, will almost certainly say that neither such a priest nor such a school-mistress as Moore depicts ever drew breath in the province of Connaught. A novelist, if he is to succeed, must make himself believed'.[7] Yet Canon Sheehan's *Luke Delmege*, in the novel of that name published four

years before Moore's, shares many traits with Moore's protagonist. Luke's history is swathed in much pious trash and
moralizing intrusions, and his problems are traced to intellectual discontent rather than to a nostalgia of the heart, but
at times we can hear in his musings too 'the mysterious
warble, soft as lake water, that abides in the heart' (1921
preface):

> Was this to be his life? Dreary days, spent in idleness and
> unprofitable attempts to raise a helpless and dispirited
> people; and dreadful evenings, when he could not escape
> from himself, but had to face the companionship of
> thoughts that verged on despair.

> The morning was fine, and a gray mist hung down over
> field and valley, and wet the withering leaves, and made
> the red haws, that splashed the whole landscape, as if
> with blood, glisten and shine. But the mist could not
> conceal the gray, lonely fields. . . 'It's a land of death
> and ruin', said Luke.[8]

Luke's affective starvation and sensitivity of temperament
produce effects at least as strange as anything experienced by
Gogarty:

> 'I have seen colouring across the moors and the breasts
> of the mountains that would make an artist's fortune,
> could he fix it on canvas. And, then, certainly the little
> children are very attractive. The one thing that strikes
> every English visitor to Ireland are the children's eyes
> — *das Vergissmeinnicht blaute Auge*!'

> Luke thought, and was tempted. He said goodbye to the
> mother, and stooping down touched with his lips the
> wet, sweet mouth of the child. He walked away, leaving
> serious wonderment in the child's mind, but infinite
> gratitude in the mother's; but he had to steady himself
> against a tree for a few moments, whilst a current of
> strange, unwonted feelings surged through his veins . . .
> it was a fatal kiss! Luke had examined his conscience
> rather too scrupulously that night, and decided that
> these little amenities were rather enervating, and were

not for him.[9]

It may be that a taboo surrounding the intimate life of the priest in rural Ireland is the reason for Gwynn's inability to recognize the precision of Moore's insight. Or it may simply be a case of that inattention to the finer resonances of the narrative against which Moore pleads in the 1921 preface: 'It may be that I heard what none other will hear . . . and it may be that all ears are not tuned, or are too indifferent or indolent to listen.' Again, a moral prejudice can utterly block awareness of what is going on in the book, so that it is read as an anti-clerical satire. It might very easily have become so, had Moore yielded to his baser instincts. What saves it from becoming so is perhaps above all the potent image of the lake itself.

The lake imposes a spell on Father Gogarty, cutting him off from his conventional existence — from Tinnick where his sisters live, just across the strait — and condemning him to an inward journey. The lake contains the secret of his identity in its bosom — symbolised by the two islands, Castle Island where he wished in youth to build a hermitage (and where George Moore's ashes now lie) and Church Island, the haunt of Marban, a saint of the times when Irish religion was still a communion with nature and with life. The secrets of this haunting and melancholy Irish landscape, secrets never laid bare, not even in the moonlight clarity of Gogarty's swim to freedom, come from a realm older and wiser than all clericalism and anticlericalism. Perhaps the lake is the indeterminate maternal principle which holds sway over all Gogarty's life, enticing him to religion with Eliza or to a flight from religion with Nora. Its grey monotony induces boredom and discontent, its subtle motions seem an invitation to escape, its magic, the magic all too rarely attaching to an individual place, commands him to remain — there is no Wagnerite who will not feel at home with such ambivalence! Later, in *The Brook Kerith*, Moore tries to evoke directly the essence of religion, and if it entirely eludes him in that work, as I fear it does, that is not only because his strategy of having a revivified Jesus repent of his apocalypticism (discovered by Weiss and Schweitzer[10]) and return to a diluted Renanism

is an unreal and academic one, but above all because the foot-
hills of Jericho and the Judean desert have no *genius loci* com-
parable to that of the Irish lakeside. Not even his Arimathean's
faintly homoerotic reveries prevent this later attempted
vision from being swallowed by the sand. In *The Lake* however the vision presses in, greater than the explicit issues of
the narrative. Yeats wrote: 'I said once: "You work so hard
that, like the Lancelot of Tennyson, you will almost see the
Grail". But now, his finished work before me, I am convinced
that he was denied even that "almost".'[11] It may be that here
is the one point at which the judgement is confuted, the one
point at which the Grail, the constant object of the aesthetic
quest, the regulative idea of a thousand revisions, is inexplic-
ably unveiled.

APPENDIX

The story which was to become 'The Wedding Gown' in *The Untilled Field* in 1903 first began its varied career as 'Grandmother's Wedding Gown' in *The Lady's Pictorial*, Christmas Number, 1887, pp. 18-20.[1]

The tale is set in a Sussex village, where Mrs. Heald (her name perhaps suggesting The Weald, which is near Horsham, a place mentioned in the story) runs a small grocery. Vixey, her daughter, has been invited to a ball at the Purdons, who are well-off tradespeople, but she does not have a suitable gown. Vixey's grandmother, who lives with them, offers the young girl her old wedding dress for the evening.

At the ball Vixey receives much attention from a youth dressed in an Elizabethan costume, who in fact tries to kiss her in a recess. She stops him but allows him to escort her home. Her grandmother had sat up to wait for her, and while doing so had looked out an old and very valuable string of pearls her dead husband had given her. The story concludes:

And the noble in blue hose and the high-waisted bride walked along the English   green; — at one end the undulating hills, at the other, the dead level of the embankment, along which the trains fled through the grey morning. He rang the bell twice, and, receiving no answer, he rang it again.

'I should have thought that would have awoke the dead', he said laughing.

'Granny is very old; she is eighty-six. She said she would sit up for me, but people sleep sound at her age'.

On trying the door, they found it had been left un-
fastened, and with fluttered hearts the sweethearts of
that evening said 'Good-bye'. One was seventeen, the
other eighteen.

'How pleased Granny will be to hear that I was
admired. What a nice young man! I hope I shall see him
again,' thought Vixey. 'Granny is, I suppose, asleep'.
Vixey opened the door, 'Oh! those are the pearls I have
been hearing about all my life; granny always said she
had forgotten what she had done with them. How
beautiful they are — how very beautiful! She is fast
asleep. How sound she does sleep. I'll try them on. 'Tis
a pity I hadn't them for the ball'.

Vixey clasped the pearls about her neck, and, encouraged by the uncouth silence in the chair, she continued her search for further treasures amid the general
lumber of the drawers. The first thing she found was a
little picture, and she stayed an exclamation of surprise;
it was as if she had passed in front of a mirror and had
seen the reflection of her face unexpectedly. Vixey
found other things — a few old fashioned rings, pieces of
a broken fan, a scent bottle; she found a will drawn up
in formal terms and duly signed: seeing her own name,
her eyes filled with tears, and when she strove to awake
Granny she was sorry, as we are sorry, for those who
outlive their day.

From *The Lady's Pictorial* (Christmas Number, 1887), pp. 18-20.

The next version of the story to be published was the translation by 'Tórna' (Taidgh O'Donoghue) in the *New Ireland
Review* (January, 1902) edited by Fr. Tom Finlay. Moore
has made many alterations in his re-working of the story for
translation into Irish. He has given it an Irish setting, naturally
enough, and changed the names of the characters. The
Healds become Muinntir Uí Dhuibhir, who have come down
in the world. Grandmother becomes Grainí Ní Chiardhubháin;
young Vixey becomes Máirín. The ball (in Irish 'rinnce') is
given by the local landowners, na Róistigh, who, though they
habitually employ Muinntir Uí Dhuibhir as servants, are
generously sensible of the fact that at one time their servants
had a higher standing in the world, that indeed these lands

were once theirs.

It will be clear then, that in translating the story from an English setting to an Irish, Moore has introduced a much greater divide between the two Irish families than that between the two English ones. But he has also introduced a sense of precariousness into the whole matter of social hierarchy: Muinntir Uí Dhuibhir were once what na Róistigh are now.[2]

This sense of the vicariousness of human fortune goes along with a much greater subtlety in the depiction of interior life in the reworked story. For example, in the version in *The Lady's Pictorial* the old grandmother often recollects the bells that rang out over the downs on her wedding day, when she wore her dress: in the Irish version Moore retains the detail of the old woman remembering the bells on the morning she got married, but this is a puzzle to everyone. We are told that it was not usual to ring the church bells for weddings. It is as if the detail from the English story assumes a ghostly (and appropriate) presence in the Irish version, emphasizing the contact the old woman has with an invisible world, the world of the dead.

The bond between the grandmother and the young girl is handled in the Irish version with much greater artistry and depth. In the first English version they are physically alike, and have a certain bond of sympathy. In the Irish version they are linked by an instinctual sensitivity, so that Máirín, at the dance, is certain that something has happened to the old woman who is waiting up for her. She goes home alone, and the writing, undistracted by Elizabethan nobles, can concentrate on her heightened awareness. There are no crass jokes about waking the dead; instead, the girl, when she lights the candle from the dying fire, *sees* the common human link between herself and the dead woman before her on the chair:

'Leig dam imtheact, a Róistigh a chara. Is dóigh liom go gcaithfead imtheacht. Táim cinnte go bhfuil rud éigint bunoscionn léi. Níor airigheas mé féin mar seo riamh roimhe seo, & ní bheinn ar an nós so muna mbeadh go bhfuil fáth éigint leis'.

'Seadh, bíodh agat, má's dultha dhuit'.

Dfhéach sí mar raibh an ghealach ag taitneamh & do rith síos an bóthar. D'fhág sí an Róisteach ag féachaint n-a ndiaidh & é 'gá cheapadh go mb'fhéidir go raibh tásg éigin fághalta aici ar bhás na sean-mhná. Oidhche bhreagh Bhealtaine do b'eadh í. Bhí gealach gheal go h-árd san spéir, & gluise an Earraigh go flúirseach ar na coilltibh & ar na bántaibh. Acht chuir cúineas na hoidhche sin sgannradh ar Mháirín, & nuair stad sí chum binn a gúna d'ardach d'airigh sí na lachain fhiadhna ag gogalaigh i measg na ngiolcach. Shíl sí ná raibh san domhan acht solas & dorchadas. Bhi sgáile dubha ar na sgeachaibh do shroicheadh na logáin bhí lán de chairr-geachaibh & de raithnigh. Ní raghadh Máirín an cosán trid an gcoill bhig ar eagla go mbuailfeadh an Bás uimpi ann, mar shíl sí gur b'amhlaidh bhí sí ag ruith ráis leis an mBás & go gcaithfeadh sí bheith ag baile roimhe. Ní raghadh sí an comhgar acht rith sí gur theip anál uirri. Tar éis tamaill do rith sí greas eile, acht ní túisge bhí sí thar an ngeata istigh 'ná bhí a fios aici go raibh buaite uirri ar an mBás. Bhuail sí fá dhó, acht ní fhuair éin-fhreagra. Annsoin do thóg sí an laiste, & tháinigh iongnadh uirri an doras do bheith gan glas air. Bhí gríosach éigint i measg na luaithreadh, a tar éis di tamall do chaitheamh gá séideadh, do las sí coinneal. Do thóg sí an choinneal i n-áirde & d'féach timcheall an tighe.

'An id' chodladh taoi a Ghrainí, no bhfuil gach éinne eile imthighthe a chodladh?'

Do dhruid si comhgarach di, & annsoin rug mian éigin fio srachta greim uirri. Nior mhaith lei riamh féachaint ar dhuine mharbh, acht anois ní raibh dul as aici; 'n-a theanta soin, is amhlaidh bhí dúil aici i bhféachaint air, & ba dhóigh léi go dtug sí fa ndeara an choslamhacht úd ar ar dtráchtadh Sean-Mhaighréad chomh minic sin.

'Go deimhin', ar sise, 'tá sí an-chosamhail liom. Bead-sa amhlaidh, lá éigint is dócha má mhairim leis'.

Annsoin do bhuail sí doras an tseomra 'n-a raibh a h-athair agus a mháthair 'n-a gcodladh.

From 'An Gúna-Phósta', 'Tórna' d'aistrigh, *New Ireland Review*, January 1902, pp. 299-310.

This, then, was the Irish version of the story which appeared in the collection entitled *An T-Úr-Ghort* in the same year from Sealy, Bryers and Walker of Dublin. Also in 1902, in April, the *English Illustrated Magazine* contained a translation, back into English, of 'Tórna's' translation of Moore's much re-worked story. This re-translation was by T.W. Rolleston, and Moore liked it. Indeed it was Moore himself who sent it to T. Fisher Unwin, who was his publisher, and who also published the *English Illustrated Magazine* at this time. On 13 March Moore wrote:

> If I were editor of a magazine I would prefer the translation to the original text. A translation from the Irish will suggest comment and (lead) to all kinds of journalistic conjecturing.[3]

Rolleston's version of the above extract from 'Torna's' version reads:

> 'Let me go, sir, please. I feel as if I have to go. I am sure that something is gone wrong with her. I never was like this before, and I would not be like this now only there was some reason for it'.
> 'All right, then; if you must, you must'.
> She looked to see if the moon was shining, and ran down the road. She left Roche looking after her, and thinking that perhaps after all she had had some premonition of the death of the old woman. It was a beautiful night in the month of May. The bright moon rode high in the sky, and the woods and fields were growing green with the bloom of springtime. But the sweetness of the night only made Maureen fear the more, and when she stopped to gather up her dress and heard the wild duck calling among the reeds, it seemed to her as if there were nothing in the world but light and darkness. Every bush cast its black shadow among the flowers and ferns by the wayside. Maureen did not

take the path through the little wood for fear that she would meet death on the way. She felt as if she were running a race with death, and that she must be home before him. She ran till she had to stop for breath, and then ran on again; but no sooner was she inside the gate than she knew that death had beaten her. She knocked twice, but no answer came. Then she lifted the latch, and wondered to find the door unlocked. There was a little glimmer in the ashes, and after blowing them for a while she lit a candle. She held the candle over her head and looked round the house.

'Is it sleeping you are Granny, or is everyone else gone to sleep?'

She went up close to her, and a certain curiosity took possession of her. She had always dreaded to look on a dead person, but now there was no getting out of it; and she even felt contented to look at her, and she seemed to trace that resemblance of which old Margaret had spoken so often.

'She is like me, surely', said Maureen. 'I suppose I will be like that some day, if I live so long'.

Then she knocked at the door of the room where her father and mother were sleeping.

'The Wedding Gown', translated from the Irish by T.W. Rolleston, *English Illustrated Magazine*, (April 1902), pp. 270-77.

The version of the story which appeared in *The Untilled Field* itself is very like Rolleston's translation. Where Moore's text does differ from Rolleston's, the differences make for greater concreteness and simplicity: the bushes become hawthorn trees; and where Maureen traced a 'resemblance' between herself and the dead woman, Molly (as she is called in the English version) sees a 'likeness'. Also Moore's writing is, understandably, more musical than Rolleston's translation. But the process of having the Irish translation translated back into English will have clarified for Moore the actuality, the physical details of his narrative. It will have made them stand clear. That clarity is to be seen in the version of the conclusion which appeared in 1903:

'Let me go, Mr. Roche; I think I must go. I feel sure that something has happened to her. I never had such a feeling before, and I could not have that feeling if there was no reason for it'.

'Well if you must go'.

She glanced to where the moon was shining and ran down the drive, leaving Mr. Roche looking after her, wondering if after all she might have had a warning of the old woman's death. The night was one of those beautiful nights in May, when the moon soars high in the sky, and all the woods and fields are clothed in the green of spring. But the stillness of the night frightened Molly, and when she stopped to pick up her dress she heard the ducks chattering in the reeds. The world seemed divided into darkness and light. The hawthorn-trees threw black shadows that reached into the hollows, and Molly did not dare to go by the path that led through a little wood, lest she should meet Death there. For now it seemed to her that she was running a race with Death, and that she must get to the cottage before him. She did not dare to take the short cut, but she ran till her breath failed her. She ran on again, but when she went through the wicket she knew that Death had been before her. She knocked twice; receiving no answer she tried the latch, and was surprised to find the door unlocked. There was a little fire among the ashes, and after blowing the sod for some time she managed to light the candle, and holding it high she looked about the kitchen.

'Auntie, are you asleep? Have the others gone to bed?'

She approached a few steps, and then a strange curiosity came over her, and though she had always feared death she now looked curiously upon death, and she thought that she saw the likeness which her aunt had often noticed.

'Yes', she said, 'she is like me. I shall be like that some day if I live long enough'.

And then she knocked at the door of the room where her parents were sleeping.

From *The Untilled Field* (London, 1903)

This achieves a fluent simplicity, a pliancy, where the narrative works into the consciousness of the young girl, as her heightened tension makes her sensitive to the natural world around her. Description is interiorized, made part of the storytelling, a technique he was to make the basis of the drama of the priest's soul in *The Lake.*

NOTES

Preface

1. See Kenneth B. Newell, ' "The Wedding Gown" Group in George Moore's *The Untilled Field*', *Éire-Ireland* (Winter, 1973), p. 71.
2. *The Letters of Evelyn Waugh* (London, 1980), edited by Mark Amory, p. 374. Mr. Rory McTurk of the University of Leeds drew my attention to this letter.
3. See Helmut E. Gerber's entry on Moore in *Anglo-Irish Literature: A Review of Research* (New York, 1976), edited by Richard J. Finneran.

George Moore's Gaelic Lawn Party by Declan Kiberd

1. *Hail and Farewell* (Colin Smythe edition, Gerrards Cross, 1976), p. 55. All further references to this edition are indicated in the text.
2. 'Literature and the Irish Language', *Ideals in Ireland*, edited by Lady Gregory (London, 1901), p. 49
3. *The Untilled Field* (Colin Smythe edition, Gerrards Cross, 1976), p. xix.
4. W.B. Yeats, 'Dramatis Personae', *Autobiographies* (London, 1955), p. 428.
5. Unpublished letter, 31 July 1901, National Library of Ireland Collection.
6. *Ideals in Ireland*, p. 51.
7. Quoted by Joseph Hone, *The Life of George Moore* (London, 1936), p. 226.
8. Ibid., p. 230.
9. Lady Gregory, *Seventy Years* (Gerrards Cross, 1974), p. 357.
10. Max Beerbohm, 'Au Revoir', *Saturday Review* (3 February, 1900); reprinted in *Around Theatres* (London, 1953), pp. 59-61.
11. 'The Irish Literary Renaissance and the Irish Language', *New Ireland Review* (April 1900), p. 66.
12. Ibid., p. 67.
13. Ibid., p. 69.
14. Ibid., p. 70.
15. 'Literature and the Irish Language', op. cit., p. 47.
16. Quoted by Alice Milligan, Letter to the Editor, *Dublin Daily Express* (21

January 1899), p. 3.

17. 'The Irish Literary Theatre — An Interview with Mr. George Moore', *Freeman's Journal* (13 November 1901), p. 5.

18. Frank Fry, *United Irishman* (11 May 1901).

19. *The Leader* (2 November 1901), p. 3.

20. *The Leader* (19 October 1907), p. 5.

21. *Freeman's Journal* (23 February 1900), p. 6.

22. *Samhain* (October 1901), p. 13.

23. 'A Plea for the Soul of the Irish People', *Nineteenth Century* (February 1901), p. 287.

24. Ibid., p. 294.

25. 'Literature and the Irish Language', op. cit., p. 48.

26. See also John Cronin, 'George Moore: The Untilled Field', *The Irish Short Story*, edited by Patrick Rafroidi and Terence Brown (Gerrards Cross, and Atlantic Highland, 1979), p. 114.

27. Quoted by Joseph Hone, *The Life of George Moore*, p. 244. See the appendix to the present volume.

28. John Eglinton, *Irish Literary Portraits* (London, 1935), pp. 87-8.

29. Quoted by Joseph Hone, *The Life of George Moore*, p. 240.

30. *J.B. Yeats: Letters to his Son W.B. Yeats and Others 1869-1922*, edited by Joseph Hone (London, 1944), p. 71.

31. *Stephen Hero*, edited by Theodore Spencer (London, 1966), p. 61.

32. *The Untilled Field*, p. 330.

33. *Letters from George Moore to Edouard Dujardin 1886-1922*, edited by John Eglinton (New York, 1929), p. 64.

34. W.B. Yeats, Letter to the Editor, *United Irishman* (24 October, 1903). See also 'J.M. Synge and the Ireland of His Time', *Essays and Introductions* (London, 1961).

35. Máirtín Ó Murchú, *Language and Community* (Dublin, 1970), p. 12.

Moore's Way Back: *The Untilled Field* and *The Lake* by Robert Welch

1. *Hail and Farewell* (Colin Smythe edition, Gerrards Cross, 1976), p. 221. All further references to this edition are indicated in the text.

2. Joseph Hone, *The Life of George Moore* (London, 1936), p. 224.

3. *The Untilled Field* (Colin Smythe edition, Gerrards Cross, 1976), p. 99. All further references to this edition are indicated in the text.

4. See John Cronin, 'George Moore: The Untilled Field' in *The Irish Short Story*, edited by Patrick Rafroidi and Terence Brown (Gerrards Cross and Atlantic Highlands, N.J., 1979), pp. 117-120. See also Helmut E. Gerber, *George Moore in Transition* (Detroit, 1968), p. 274.

5. McCabe is supposed by some to be modelled on Gerald O'Donovan, a Catholic priest who left the priesthood and became a novelist. See the Macmillan *Dictionary of Irish Literature* edited by Robert Hogan (London, 1980), p. 509.

6. W.B. Yeats, *Autobiographies* (London, 1970 edition), p. 343.

7. 'the real McCabe' is an Hiberno-Irish phrase I have often heard my father use to attest ironically to someone's or something's authenticity. A comic distortion of 'the real McCoy'?

8. See Richard Cave, *A Study of the Novels of George Moore* (Gerrards Cross, 1978), p. 133.

9. *The Lake* (Colin Smythe edition, Gerrards Cross, 1980), p. 179. All further references to this edition are indicated in the text.

Turgenev and Moore: *A Sportsman's Sketches* and *The Untilled Field* by Richard Allen Cave

1. Quoted in J.M. Hone, *The Life of George Moore* (London, 1936), p. 246.

2. *Hail and Farewell* (Colin Smythe edition, Gerrards Cross, 1976), pp. 346-7.

3. 'Turgueneff', *The Fortnightly Review* (February, 1888), pp. 247-8.

4. Henry James: 'Ivan Turgenieff', *French Poets and Novelists* (London, 1878), p. 285.

5. Edward Garnett, *Turgenev* (London, 1927), p. ix of the introduction by Joseph Conrad.

6. 'Turgueneff', *The Fortnightly Review*, p. 241.

7. All references to *A Sportsman's Sketches* included in the text are to the translation in two volumes by Constance Garnett of 1896. This, while being contemporary to Moore's work, is still the most accessible and the fullest translation of the tales; a more recent translation by Richard Freeborn (Harmondsworth, 1967) is of only a selection of the stories.

8. Henry James, op. cit., p. 283.

9. Ibid., p. 282.

10. Ibid., p. 292.

11. George Moore, 'Turgueneff', *The Fortnightly Review*, p. 240.

12. Ibid., pp. 242 and 247.

13. It is invariably difficult to choose a definitive text for one of Moore's works and *The Untilled Field* is no exception, though there are fewer variant versions than with some of his publications. Throughout this essay all references are to the revised second English edition published by Heinemann in 1914, reprinted with a foreword by T.R. Henn (Gerrards Cross, 1976), as this contains Moore's preferred versions of most of the stories and in an order which he did not subsequently change. A later footnote discusses texts of 'The Wild Goose' when the tale is under discussion, as that merits rather special consideration.

14. George Moore, 'Since the Elizabethans', *Cosmopolis* (October, 1896), p. 56. The phrase occurs in a discussion about another Russian novelist, Tolstoy.

15. Henry James, op. cit., p. 292.

16. Rosa Mulholland, 'The Hungry Death', *Representative Irish Tales*, edited by W.B. Yeats, 1891, reprinted with a foreword by M.H. Thuente (Gerrards Cross, 1979), pp. 329-30.

17. Ibid., p. 292.

18. George Moore, 'Turgueneff', p. 240.

19. V.S. Pritchett, *The Gentle Barbarian: The Life and Work of Turgenev* (London,

1977), p. 58.

20. Constance Garnett has given a particularly flat, even trite-sounding translation here, evoking suggestions of childish enthusiasm in the word 'wonderful' that are wholly absent from the Russian original. Freeborn offers 'astonishing' which gets the right connotations of the extraordinary, though there is still a somewhat melodramatic quality about it which he successfully avoids at the end of the tale when he turns the phrase on its repetition into the idea, more colloquial and down-to-earth in its expression, that 'Russians surprise one when it comes to dying'. Charrière's French translation which is the version in which Moore read the *Sketches* contrives to hit on an idiom that at once intimates an ordinary everyday occurrence, and yet something uniquely individual: Russians, he writes, have 'une manière à eux de mourir'.

21. 'Hor and Kalinitch', the first of the *Sketches*, established the pattern here, which Turgenev returned to frequently. Hor is the shrewd, worldly, successful farmer whose imagination never strays beyond his fields; Kalinitch, the imaginative peasant, enormously skilled in local lore, ever curious about other people, ways of life and customs and quite without a thought for his material well-being. Each respects the other and depends on that respect considerably; neither is viewed by the narrator to the other's detriment.

22. 'The Wild Goose' exists in several versions; that referred to here is the expanded and revised text printed with *The Untilled Field* in 1914 and reprinted in the 1976 edition. The first edition of 1903 is largely the same text in the body of the story and the same criticism applies to it as is given here; for the 1914 edition Moore expanded facets of the narrative especially the opening account of Carmady's past and the events leading to his first meeting with Ellen. The tale met with considerable criticism and in 1926 Moore revised it once again, this time shortening it, concentrating more on Ellen and how her temperament brings about the collapse of her marriage with Carmady; but the opinionating remains, though it is somewhat toned down, the sweeping generalisations about the only way in which Ireland can expect to have a future challenging and irritating the reader as none of the other tales do. Moore refused to omit the tale altogether, claiming in a prefatory note to the 1926 edition that it was dearer to him personally than the other stories that precede it. This perhaps in part explains the problems one has with the piece as it clearly contains an amount of poorly digested autobiographical material (both in the actual opinions expressed and in the setting which is almost certainly Tymon Lodge, Tallaght, Clara Christian's home near Dublin) which was to find a more suitable context for its development in *Hail and Farewell*.

'Fugitives' was a story composed for the 1931 edition of *The Untilled Field* constructed out of two shorter tales, 'In the Clay' and 'The Way Back', which had framed the collection as first and last of the stories in the first edition of 1903. That was published by Fisher Unwin in April of that year; the Continental edition issued the following month omitted those two tales as Moore had grown (rightly) dissatisfied with them immediately on publication and they were omitted from the subsequent editions until 1931. The stories, in whichever form, seem something of a throw-back to the style of *Evelyn Innes* (she, in fact, with Sir Owen Asher and Harding, the novelist, actually appears in the narrative). Essentially the tales concern the superiority of a group of super-sophisticates to the cultural life of Dublin; their nervous, intellectual 'brilliance' does not appear to the reader as attractive as Moore clearly intends it to; the suggestion that theirs is an ideal life to which the Irish might aspire is a sad failure of judgement on his part.

23. See *Hail and Farewell*, p. 352; and *George Moore in Transition; Letters to T. Fisher Unwin and Lena Milman*, edited by H.E. Gerber (Detroit, 1968), pp. 267-71. This was the one tale the publisher expressed any concern over, requesting Moore to think of revising it. Though the discussion between them tended to focus on the 'morality' of including the scene where Ellen suckles her baby but eventually agrees to hire a wet nurse to meet her husband's wishes when he expresses fears that she will lose her figure, Fisher Unwin clearly was uneasy about the whole story. Gerber is excellent in his account of the growth of Moore's anti-clerical fervour and how it is reflected in the correspondence with his publishers.

24. For a more detailed study of the conclusion of this tale see the 'Afterword' to my edition of Moore's *The Lake* (Gerrards Cross, 1980, pp. 205-6). See also the appendix to the present volume.

25. 'Julia Cahill's Curse' which follows 'A Playhouse in the Waste' continues the device of the jarvey's chatter about strange occurrences in the neighbourhood and is one instance of Moore's use of the atmosphere created by one story to help rapidly achieve an appropriate mood for the next. In the 1903 edition 'Julia Cahill's Curse' came between the two stories about Father McTurnan; the later ordering is infinitely preferable since each tale then makes a more creative use of the mood evoked at the close of the preceding one. After the subtleties of 'A Playhouse in the Waste', Moore does not need to create an intricate structure within the narrative to induce the reader to take apparently supernatural events seriously; simply continuing the characters of the traveller and the jarvey from the previous tale into the opening of this one is sufficient to suspend our disbelief. The narrative devices of the first story are by implication at work still in this.

26. Gustave Flaubert, *Letters* (London, 1950), selected with an introduction by Richard Rumbold and translated by J.M. Cohen, p. 140.

27. Ibid., p. 240.

A Naked Gael Screaming 'Brian Boru' by Tomás Ó Murchadha

1. *Hail and Farewell* (Colin Smythe edition, Gerrards Cross, 1976), p. 111. All further references to this edition are indicated in the text.
2. *The Lake* (Colin Smythe edition, Gerrards Cross, 1980), p. x. All further references to this edition are indicated in the text.
3. *The Untilled Field* (Colin Smythe edition, Gerrards Cross, 1976), p. xvii. All further references to this edition are indicated in the text.
4. *The Brook Kerith* (London, 1931 edition), pp. 461-2.

George Moore's *The Lake*: A Possible Source by John Cronin

1. Reprinted, with the author's permission, and by kind consent of the journal, from *Eire-Ireland*, Fall 1971, pp. 12-15.
2. pp. 10-11. The pamphlet has been placed in the library of the Queen's University, Belfast.
3. *The Lake* (London, 1905), p. 274. All further references to this edition are indicated in the text.
4. Joseph Hone, *The Life of George Moore* (London, 1936), p. 247.
5. '(An Irish Priest to his Flock). Lettere di vu ex-prete catolico romano alla sua greggia', pp. 23. Firenze, 1889. See *British Museum General Catalogue of Printed Books* (London, 1966), Vol. 42, p. 1111.
6. Fr. Connellan surfaces again briefly in the 'Lestrygonians' chapter of Joyce's *Ulysses* when Leopold Bloom passes his bookstore and remarks in the window the significant titles *Why I left the Church of Rome. Birds Nest* (*Ulysses*, Penguin edition, p. 180).

The Continuous Melody of *The Lake* by Clive Hart

1. *The Lake*, 2nd impression (London, November 1905) p. 309. All further references to this edition are indicated in the text.
2. As Moore points out in the dedication to the novel, he took the title of Ellis's book, *The Source of the Christian River*, from Edouard Dujardin's *La source du fleuve chretien: histoire critique du judaisme ancien et du christianisme primitif* (Paris, 1906), on which Dujardin was working at the time.
3. See Charles Joseph Burkhart, *The Letters of George Moore to Edmund Gosse, W.B. Yeats, R.I. Best, Miss Nancy Cunard, and Mrs. Mary Hutchinson* (Ann Arbor, 1974), p. 301. (Xerographic copy, from microfilm, of a doctoral dissertation for the University of Maryland, 1958.)

Siegfried in Ireland: A Study of Moore's *The Lake* by Max E. Cordonnier

1. Reprinted by kind consent of the journal, from *The Dublin Magazine* (Spring, 1967), pp. 3-12.
2. *The Lake* (Colin Smythe edition, Gerrards Cross, 1980), p. x. All further references to this edition are indicated in the text.
3. *Letters to Lady Cunard, 1895-1933*, edited by Rupert Hart-Davis (London, 1957), p. 45.
4. Moore's friend Dujardin called Wagner's method of repetitive motifs the parent of the interior monologue: 'le motif wagnerien est une phrase isolée qui comporte toujours une signification emotionelle, mais qui n'est pas reliée logiquement à celles qui précèdent et à celles qui suivant, et c'est en cela que le monologue interieur en procède. . .' *Le Monologue Intérieur, Son Apparition, Ses Origines, Sa Place Dans L'Oeuvre de James Joyce* (Paris, 1931), pp. 54-5.
5. Thomas Mann, 'The Sufferings and Greatness of Richard Wagner', *Essays*

(New York, 1957), p. 203.

6. Dujardin, *Le Monologue Interieur*, p. 18.

7. Ibid., p. 17.

8. *Sigmund Freud, A General Introduction to Psychoanalysis* (New York, 1956), p. 80.

9. See, for example, Kate Ede's delirious death-bed scene at the end of *A Mummer's Wife*; Maggie Brookes's somnambulistic nightmare in *Spring Days*; Evelyn Innes's erotic nightmare in *Sister Teresa*; Heloise's peaks of tension in *Heloise and Abelard*.

10. Thomas Mann, *Essays*, p. 204.

11. *Sister Teresa* (New York, 1923), p. 255.

12. *Hail and Farewell* (Colin Smythe edition, Gerrards Cross, 1976), p. 609.

Father Bovary by John Stephen O'Leary

1. See Georg Lukács, *Die Theorie des Romans* (Berlin, 1965), part two, Chapter II, on 'The Novel of Disillusion'. For the 'capitalization of spirit' in Balzac, see: *Studies in European Realism: a sociological survey of the writings of Balzac, Stendhal, Zola, Tolstoy, Gorki and Others* (London, 1950).

2. J. Hillis Miller, *The Disappearance of God: Five Nineteenth Century Writers* (Harvard, 1963), p. 11.

3. Stephane Mallarme, 'Quant au livre', *Oeuvres Completes* (Pleiade, 1965), p. 378.

4. See also Eileen Kennedy, 'Design in George Moore's *The Lake*' in *Modern Irish Literature*, edited by Raymond J. Porter and James D. Brophy (New York, 1972), which examines Moore's patterning of nature symbolism in the 1905 edition of *The Lake*.

5. *The Lake* (Colin Smythe edition, Gerrards Cross, 1980), p. 140. All further references to this edition are indicated in the text.

6. The symbolism of dawn probably owes something to the dawn scene in *Gotterdammerung*, as the phrase 'blow a horn on the hillside to call comrades together' in the same letter recalls Siegfried's horn call in that scene. Thus where the symbolism of the exposition recalled *Siegfried*, Act II, in which the still adolescent hero seeks his way to Brünnhilde, the symbolism of the recapitulation alludes to the scene in which Siegfried has become a man, ready to leave Brünnhilde in order to confront the world at large. Moore claimed that the style of *The Lake* owed much to his frequent listening to the *Lohengrin* prelude. The movement from indeterminate vagueness to dazzling radiance and back to dreamlike vagueness again, which we may note in Moore's treatment of lake and sky (and of the priest's soul), is certainly reminiscent of that music. Wagner's programme note reads: 'Out of the clear blue ether of the sky there seems to condense a wonderful yet at first hardly perceptible vision; and out of this there gradually emerges, ever more and more clearly, an angel-host bearing in its midst the sacred Grail'. Another Wagnerian note: Siegfried first learns fear as he trembles when approaching Brünnhilde; Parsifal learns of sorrow and compassion from Kundry's kiss. That there is a Wagnerian character in Gogarty's awakening is suggested by the following: 'There have been

cases of men and women going mad because their love was not reciprocated, and I used to listen to these stories wonderingly, unable to understand, bored by the relation' (page 126). Like Parsifal, Gogarty was a 'pure fool' and has become 'knowing through compassion'. It is in this Wagnerian tonality that we should hear the remark Gogarty lets drop in an amusing conversation with Moran: 'Woman is life' (page 230).

7. Stephen Gwynn, *Irish Literature and Drama* (New York, 1936), pp. 168-9.
8. Canon Sheehan, *Luke Delmege* (London, 1901), pp. 343 and 332-3.
9. Ibid., pp. 348 and 360.
10. See Albert Schweitzer, *The Quest of the Historical Jesus* (London, 1954), pp. 237-40 and pp. 180-92.
11. W.B. Yeats, *Autobiographies* (London, 1970 edition), p. 438.

Appendix

1. See Helmut E. Gerber, *George Moore in Transition* (Detroit, 1968), pp. 236-7n, where Gerber draws attention to the version of 'The Wedding Gown' in the *Lady's Pictorial*.
2. This situation is analagous to that which obtains between the Barfields and the Latches in *Esther Waters* (1894). See Wayne E. Hall, *Shadowy Heroes* (New York, 1980), p. 102.
3. *George Moore in Transition*, p. 248.

NOTES ON THE ESSAYISTS

Cave, Richard Allen, lectures in the Department of English at Bedford College in the University of London and is Director of the University's International Summer School for Graduates. Dr. Cave's publications include *A Study of the Novels of George Moore* (1978) and editions of Moore's *Hail and Farewell* (1976) and *The Lake* (1980). He is Honorary Secretary of the Consortium for Drama and Media in Higher Education and General Editor of the series *Theatre in Focus* to which he has contributed the volume *Terence Gray and the Festival Theatre Cambridge* (1980).

Cordonnier, Max E., Professor of English at Southeast Missouri State University at Cape Girardeau. He took his doctorate at the University of Kansas in 1965. He has edited a poetry magazine, *The Cape Rock Journal*, writes poetry and is a regular reviewer for *Choice*.

Cronin, John, Professor of English at the Queen's University, Belfast. A Corkman, he previously lectured at the University of the Witwatersrand, Johannesburg. He is the author of *Somerville and Ross* (Bucknell, 1972), *Gerald Griffin 1803-1840: A Critical Biography* (Cambridge, 1978) and *The Anglo-Irish Novel: Vol. 1, The Nineteenth Century* (Belfast, 1980). He is Chairman of the Committee for the Study of Anglo-Irish Literature at the Royal Irish Academy.

Hart, Clive, born in Perth, Western Australia, 1931. Educated at the University Western Australia, Paris and Cambridge. Professor of English at Dundee, now Professor of Literature at the University of Essex. Author of a number of books on James Joyce, kites, and the prehistory of aviation. Editor of John Webster's tragedies. Trustee of the James Joyce Foundation.

Kiberd, Declan, lectures in Anglo-Irish Literature and Drama at University College, Dublin. He has held posts as Lecturer in Irish at Trinity College, Dublin and as Lecturer in English at the University of Kent at Canterbury. He was Prendergast Scholar at Oxford University where he wrote a doctoral dissertation, subsequently published as *Synge and the Irish Language* (1979). His next book will be a study of Joyce, Beckett and Ó Cadhain under the title *The Last Europeans*.

O'Leary, Joseph Stephan, born in Cork, 1949; has pursued studies in French and English Literature, philosophy and theology in Maynooth, Rome and Paris. A theologian, he has written on Heidegger, Proust and Henry James. He is co-editor of *Heidegger et la question de Dieu* (1980) and is at present lecturing in theology at the University of Notre Dame.

Ó Murchadha, Tomás, spent some time in the Abbey Theatre, where he produced a number of successful plays. Now a full time writer, he lives on Mangerton in Co. Kerry, writes a column for the *Cork Examiner* and broadcasts occasionally. Has written two novels which still await publishers and is at work on a third.

Welch, Robert, lectures in the School of English, University of Leeds, where he is co-organizer of the M.A. in Anglo-Irish Literature. His publications include *Irish Poetry from Moore to Yeats* (1980) and various writings in Irish and English. Poetry reviewer for the *Yorkshire Post*. At present at work on a *Companion to Irish Literature*.

INDEX

(The notes are not indexed).

137